To remind you of Jan. '84.
Fondest Love
Stuart & Lenette.

CAPE TOWN
THE FAIREST CAPE

CAPE TOWN
THE FAIREST CAPE

PETER SCHIRMER

PHOTOGRAPHS BY
HERMAN POTGIETER
AND
CLOETE BREYTENBACH

C. STRUIK (PTY) LTD

AUTHOR'S ACKNOWLEDGEMENTS

Generations of scholars and historians have attributed the over-worked quotation 'the fairest Cape. . .' to Sir Francis Drake, but it was in fact penned by the mandatory cleric who sailed with the *Golden Hind.* This gentleman of the cloth is long since forgotten and Drake is remembered – except by South African school children – for other things, yet this generally held misconception serves to underscore how easy it is for the researcher to accept as 'fact' an initial error which has been perpetuated by repetition. In preparing this manuscript Miss M. George, of the South African Archives in Cape Town, was able through her own knowledge and extensive research to guide me around many such pitfalls and introduce me to many little known facts. Interpretation of the facts – unless indicated in the text – is my own, and Miss George shares no responsibility for any faulty or controversial argument; I do, however, owe her a very great debt of gratitude for her advice, help, encouragement and time.

It is fitting, too (and an appropriate come-uppance for my male chauvinism), that in writing of the 'Mother City' my other debt of gratitude should be to three more ladies, all of whom hold very special places in my affections: my former colleague René Gordon, who is missed for her companionship as much as her distinctive flair for books, gave encouragement; Marje Hemp, whose love of the more obscure events and byways of our history echoes my own, and who curbed, with gentle sense, my worst flights of fancy; and last, but not least, my wife Jill who firmly curbed my daughters' more excessive verbal fights through the long hours of putting the manuscript together. A special word of thanks to Brenda Reinders who not only interpreted my scrawl and corrected my grammar, but whose enthusiasm for the text encouraged me to continue when the other Muses took time off to have their hair done.

For them then – and the other enchanting daughters of the Mother City: Eva, Hottentot Nell, Portuguese Rosie – I echo the arcane toast 'The Ladies. . . God Bless 'em'.

Peter Schirmer

PHOTOGRAPHER'S ACKNOWLEDGEMENT

Mr Dave Aronovitz of Frank and Hirsch for the loan of Nikon lenses.
Herman Potgieter

Published by C. Struik (Pty) Ltd, Struik House, Oswald Pirow Street, Foreshore, Cape Town

First edition: 1983

Copyright: Text © Peter Schirmer
Photographs © Herman Potgieter and Cloete Breytenbach

Design by Walther Votteler, Cape Town
Dustjacket design by Janice Ashby Design Studio, Cape Town
Photoset by McManus Bros (Pty) Ltd, Cape Town
Lithographic reproduction by Hirt & Carter (Pty) Ltd, Cape Town
Printed and bound by South China Printing Co., Hong Kong

Photographic credit: Photographs no 27, 28, 30, 49, 88 and 110 were taken by J.R. Dickson, Cape Town.

ISBN 0 86977 186 8

1 *(title page). Under a cloudscape that would be the envy of any artist, the rocky bastions of the Mother City – Table Mountain, Devil's Peak and Lion's Head – are still in shadow, though the early morning sun already blesses the centre of Cape Town with the promise of a fine summer's day.*
2. *Against the backdrop of Signal Hill, the concrete and glass blocks of modern skyscrapers rise in sharp contrast to the sprawl of the pointed pentacle that is the Castle. Separated in time by three eventful centuries, only the dwindling space of the Grand Parade keeps old and new apart.*
3 *(overleaf). Dusk brings a fairyland quality to the city and its suburbs as the rainbow colours of neon advertising vie with the street lights to diminish the gathering dark. And as greater Cape Town grows, stretching ever further – as here, across the Cape Flats and out towards the 'northern' suburbs – so the tide of lights flows with it.*
4. *Softened by evening's shadows, which can touch even a Victorian pillar box with glamour, Adderley Street retains something of its hectic daytime bustle – heightened to a frenzy for three weeks each autumn by the Cape Town Festival, whose emblems adorn the old lamp standards of this, the city centre's main commercial artery.*

CONTENTS

Author's acknowledgements 4

The Looming Giant 11
Kirstenbosch 30

The Tavern of the Seas 35
Cape Point 65

Robben Island 68

A Meltingpot of People 71
District Six 96

History's Lasting Fabric 101
The Arts 128

The Boland 131

Index 144

THE LOOMING GIANT

Even today, when elevated freeways mar its shoreline, Cape Town is best approached from the sea. . . from west of north, just as its founders did when they came in their tiny wooden ships. In those days of sail it was customary for a captain to reward the first man to sight Table Mountain. . . with brandy, a silver piece, or even a golden ducat if landfall had been particularly anxious.

For the modern voyager, the sight of the flat-topped mountain and its attendant peaks is reward enough. In autumn or early spring their earliest indication is a cotton-wool puff of cloud resting first where sky and sea meet, then lifting above the horizon, and followed some sea miles later by the blue-grey smudge of the massif itself. In winter its discovery is even more dramatic: it materializes suddenly from the cloud-wrapped shore, bulking so close that one feels one could almost stretch out to touch the sandstone of the precipitous mountain face frowning down on the city.

But in summer the mountain is flushed with the reds and golds of early morning and smiles a welcome. Wavelets dance a sparkling greeting across Table Bay and gulls screech their raucous 'ave'. And if the Southeaster blows, the mountain may well wear its wig – *la perruque* to the French mariners, but better known today as the Tablecloth; and the returning Capetonian will recognize with gladness that Van Hunks and the Devil continue their age-old smoking contest.

The advent of the jet airliner and the disappearance of the old mailship service have deprived most visitors of this, one of the world's most spectacular landfalls. Only yachtsmen, mariners, cruise ship passengers and a dwindling handful of trawlermen still share its winter splendour so aptly described by Lady Anne Barnard in 1797 and – despite the impositions of modern man – essentially so little changed since then. Lady Anne, an observer as deft with charcoal and brush as she was with her pen, was a prodigious letter-writer and left a splendid record of the social scene during her brief years as the settlement's 'First Lady'. Of her arrival she wrote:

'. . .the joyfull news of *land* being seen was announced, tho it was enveloped in such fogs as did not permit us to enjoy its appearance till we were exactly placed in the bay opposite to Cape Town – then, as if by one consent the Lions rump whisked off the vapours with its tail; the Lions Head untyed and dropd, the necklace of clouds w^c surrounded its erect throat, & table mountain over which a white damask table cloth had been spread half way down showd its broad face & smiled, while guns from the garrison & from all the batterys, welcomed his Majesty's government, & the distant hills who could not step foward to declare their allegiance, by the awefull thunders of their acquiescing echoes, informed us that they were not ignorant of the arrival of the governor who was at that moment putting his foot on Land.'

Lady Anne arrived at the Cape in May and, like so many visitors before and since, came immediately under the mountain's brooding spell – nothing would suffice but that she should climb it. And climb it she did, though not until July, and in spite of protests from local society that no lady worth the name had ever made the ascent – a claim which Lady Anne records with a sensible pinch of salt. She had difficulty, too, in persuading any of her new acquaintances to accompany her – a reluctance which she put down to their 'lazyness' but which, given normal July rainfall, was probably prudence prevailing over chivalry on the part of both the knowledgeable burghers and the officers of the British garrison, a prudence with which any sensible Capetonian will sympathize.

But in John Barrow, explorer and chronicler extraordinary, she found a soul as venturesome as herself and, on one of those halcyon days which still compensate for the gloom of the Peninsula's winter, she 'braved the cliffs'. A brace of young naval officers impressed from a ship in the Bay and a retinue of servants accompanied the stocky Barrow and the svelte First Lady. Their route to the 'Front Table' and the massif's highest point was up Platteklip Gorge, the deep cleft that gashes the sheer face overlooking the city.

Heavy bush and tangled vines clothing the lower slopes hamper the approach to the foot of the gorge. From there it is a steep scramble rather than a

5 (previous page). *Though the sandstone and granite spine of the Peninsula and its white-lace tracery of waves offer constantly-changing perspectives and vistas of beauty, only from the air is its full magnificence apparent.*
6. *Perched eyrie-like above the city's sprawl, the upper cable station looms through wraiths of cloud, dwarfing the red-roofed passenger car on its upward journey – one of a pair which in a five-minute climb or descent can carry up to 28 passengers to or from the summit. It is from this, the highest building in the Peninsula – 1 067 m above sea level – that the cars' movements are controlled as they travel at 17 km/h along the 1 244 m cableway between the upper and lower cable stations, separated by a vertical distance of 701 m.*

7. *Legend has it that the cotton-wool blanket of cloud, which the South-easter tumbles over the mountain's crest, pours from the long clay pipes smoked by the Devil and Van Hunks in a contest which began centuries ago on the upper slopes of Devil's Peak – then still known as the Wÿndberg. Van Hunks, a retired pirate married to a viperish harridan, would frequently escape her nagging tongue to the quiet of the slopes and a contemplative pipe. On one such occasion he was accosted by a stranger who asked to share his 'baccy' pouch and, when the two were smoking contentedly, claimed he could puff greater clouds of smoke than the former pirate. To the Devil's consternation, the old rogue's lungs proved just as powerful as his own; and so the pair are locked in competition to this day.*

French mariners, unaware of the contest, dubbed their smoke le perruque, or wig; later, English sea-captains ignored the Devil's presence on the slopes and called the rich white smoke 'the Tablecloth'.

climb, but made tricky by the litter of water-smoothed stones that threaten to turn an unwary ankle. Even in winter the scramble soon becomes taxing, creates a thirst – which Lady Anne and her party quenched liberally with port, diluted with the icy water that cascades from Plattekloof's rocky walls.

That early ascent seems to have been fairly leisurely, with frequent pauses for Barrow to chip off pieces of rock, using a hammer with which Lady Anne had come equipped – either fortuitously, or because she had forewarning of 'the good Mr B.'s' penchant to stray from the project at hand into the pursuit of his private researches.

This route was the one taken by Antonio de Saldanha, the Portuguese navigator who in 1503 made the first recorded climb, naming the sandstone and granite giant *Taboa do Cabo*. But his approach and ascent must have been far more taxing than that of Lady Anne's party, for the slopes and even the mountain itself were then densely covered in indigenous vegetation – thorny bushes, creepers and almost impenetrable thickets of leucadendron and protea barred the passage of these first white men to thrust towards, and then up, Platteklip. Furthermore, De Saldanha was faced with the uncertainty of what lay at the top let alone what dangers might beset his passage. The Barnard-Barrow party followed an already well-established route – the many pieces of soles and heel leather which Lady Anne remarked bear testimony to this, even as rusting tins and plastic containers mark the litter-strewn route today.

Despite the retinue of bearers, their jaunt was not so much an exploration, or even adventure, as a picnic, and Lady Anne records with mouth-watering and Water-Rat thoroughness the spread of cold meats and wines with which they celebrated their conquest.

Nearly three centuries separated the ascent by De Saldanha's explorers and the society picnickers, but both parties seem to have been more fascinated by the staggering views from the table top than the vast botanical treasure-house spread literally at their feet. Saldanha used the opportunity offered by the panorama of the Peninsula, the Cape Flats and the curves of Table and False bays to correct and detail his sketchy charts. To Lady Anne the bird's-eye view was of 'the formal meanness of its [Cape Town's] appearance which would have led us to suppose it built by children out of half dozen packs of cards.'

A far cry from her strenuous but pleasant climb was that of a contemporary, but infinitely more reluctant, visitor to the Cape. This was Joshua Penny, a New Yorker who had the misfortune to be press-ganged into the Royal Navy to serve on *HMS Sceptre*. When his ship put in to Table Bay in 1799, Penny made his way ashore, hid until nightfall in the bush which still fringed the fledgling town, and then made his escape up the mountain – to freedom, if not necessarily safety.

In anticipation of flight he had equipped himself with a stout seaman's knife, a flint and steel – and very little else. After two days he found a small dry cave

8

9

beside a stream high on the western side of the mountain and in an area he described as 'teeming' with wild animals – which were to provide his main diet, and eventually clothes, for the next 14 months.

In the account of his Robinson Crusoe existence, published in 1815, he writes: 'My clothes, by creeping through the rocks and bushes, were so tattered that I had become almost naked. In this extremity I made a needle from the bone of a beast, the eye of which being made with my sharp pointed knife, enabled me to sew with the sinews of my antelopes. With my skins I equipped myself completely from head to foot.'

From the earliest days of settlement the mountain had provided a usually-brief refuge for runaway slaves and deserters. But its upper plateaux are not particularly hospitable – not even a roaring brushwood fire can entirely dispel the damp winter chill of even the most protected caves. The isolation of the summit and the effort required to attain it, as well as the relative inaccessibility of the abundance of sea-shore foods, will have contributed to its being shunned by early Stone Age people. This had little changed and Penny, who made one brief descent to collect shell-fish at today's Camps Bay, records:

'During my residence I had never been able to discover the vestige of a human being, except myself, having ventured here.' The loneliness of his long sojourn, keeping tally of the passage of time by cutting a notch into a stick each full moon, will have been compounded by fear of discovery. Did he ever regret exchanging the hell of a frigate's foc'sle for his solitary existence as the mountain's first true 'bergie'? Penny makes no comparison in his account. But his spell as a hunter-gatherer hermit was very different to that of his modern counterparts, who combine a vinous and spirited cameraderie with a beggar-scavenger way of life.

In the event, loneliness told. Unkempt and skin-clad, he made his way down, taking a circuitous route between the town and its neighbouring 'suburb' of Papendorp (now Woodstock). He reached the beach unobserved and hid among the dunes until he spotted the captain of a barque being rowed ashore.

16

'I tried my power of speech to prepare myself. The captain landing advanced guardedly towards me, I stepped up to meet him and asked him if he wanted to ship a man? He was surprised to hear me speak and asked: "What in the name of God are you! Man or beast?" He at last stepped up to me and giving me his hand said "this is no place to talk – jump into the boat and go on board." The boat was ordered to return for him in half an hour; into it I sprung and was soon snug aboard.'

When Penny's account of his adventures was published as a pamphlet in the United States in 1815 it was greeted with some scepticism, while the townsfolk of Cape Town mocked it as a 'total fabrication'. However, in 1894 a party of climbers at the top of Woody Ravine found the ragged remnants of a buckram sailor's jacket, a hat-band and a striking-steel which were pronounced to have been Penny's and which lent some credibility to his tale. By then the mountain had become positively over-populated compared with Penny's day; not only had the late Victorians – otherwise noted for their shyness of fresh air – taken to the 'gentlemanly sport of mountaineering' with ungenteel gusto, but a 470-strong workforce was housed within a few hundred metres of the absconding seaman's refuge.

Yet so well hidden was Penny's cave that, for all the later to-ing and fro-ing, its existence remained uncertain until the late 1940s. The find, beneath a detritus of decaying leaves and animal droppings, of a second steel, the remnants of a corroded knife, a belt-buckle, the bowls of two clay pipes and rags of clothing, as well as a plethora of charred bones, confirmed the legend as fact.

The shelter was little more than a deep overhang, camouflaged by a centuries-old tangle of bush and creepers, and – unlike some of the mountain's other caves – hardly worthy of the name. Some of the latter have never been fully explored, for parts of the massif are honey-combed with pipes and water-eroded chambers formed long before the last ice age left its signature in the stone visitors' book which paves the surround of McClear's Beacon. Pools of great but uncertain depth mark the floors of some of these subterranean pits and in their black waters a remarkable range of aquatic creatures – crustaceans, insects and even fish – live their cycle of existence in everlasting dark.

Deep underground they mirror the immemorial conflict of predator and prey which continues on the surface, infinitely better lit but only slightly more public. For though all the large predators, and most of the large raptors, have disappeared from the mountain and its environs, a host of smaller creatures continue Nature's shambles with tooth and talon, claw and mandible.

When Van Riebeeck and his small group of pioneer settlers set out to tame the land of *Tafel Vallei* and its vicinity, creating the nucleus of what was to become Cape Town, leopards still stalked the crags and ledges of the mountain; the now-extinct Cape lion – though never many of them – prowled the slopes and on occasion raided the fringes of the cantonment, making off with livestock; and hyenas, their eyes 'glowing in the firelight like the coals of Satan's pit' made the night raucous with their cries.

Even in Barrow's day there was a wealth of wildlife which has long since disappeared from the Peninsula. The lion were no more and leopard were rare, but 'the wooded kloofs or clefts in the mountain still give shelter to the few remaining troops of wolves [jackals?] and hyenas that not many years ago were very troublesome to the town'. And later he records: 'The larger kinds of birds that hover round the summit of the Table Mountain are vultures, eagles, kites and crows that assist the wolves in cleansing the country near the town of a nuisance that is tacitly permitted by the police.'

Barrow was a fastidious gentleman, at least in so far as the habits of others were concerned, and the 'nuisance' to which he refers was the 'offal from slaughter-houses that are shamefully suffered to be left or thrown even at the sides of public roads'.

None of the larger species of antelope browsed even the lower slopes of Table Mountain, but its kloofs and plateaux were still home to substantial numbers of duiker and grysbok (the latter causing 'no small damage at night to

10

The silhouette from which Table Mountain's name derives is misleading, for the top with its panoramic view of the city spread between the massif's lower slopes and Table Bay (8) is, in fact, a series of plateaux broken by rocky outcrops and sandy slopes forming catchment areas for a series of reservoirs (9), which for many years provided most of the city's water. As man has encroached, so the mountain's wild creatures have dwindled, though that unlikely relative of the elephant, the inquisitive and ubiquitous dassie (10) continues to thrive.

11 *(overleaf). From Constantia Nek at the head of the once-fabled Valley of the Vines, the 'back' of Table Mountain offers an ever-changing aspect as it sweeps upwards through prim forests to the rougher world of fynbos and, eventually, to the rugged face seen from the city or the shale outcrop of Robben Island, standing sentinel in the bay.*

*When, in 1895, Cecil Rhodes commissioned the Scots sculptor John Tweed to execute a statue of Jan van Riebeeck for a £1 000 fee, he stipulated that the work – one of the empire-builder's many gifts to the Mother City – remain unsigned. Perhaps this was as well, for the result (**12**) was not only inaccurate in terms of dress, but artistically mediocre. Nevertheless, the finished statue commanded pride of place when four years later it was unveiled at the head of the old main pier. Today, dwarfed by the modern megaliths of the city he founded and patinaed by its grime, Van Riebeeck surveys the Heerengracht and man's other handiworks that bridge three centuries of endeavour.*

*Oldest of these works still extant is the reservoir built by Van Riebeeck's successor, Zacharias Wagenaar, in the bed of the Fresh River to ensure a constant supply of drinking water for passing ships. The reservoir (**14**), which was uncovered during excavations for the Golden Acre complex where it has been retained in situ, gave Wagenaar none of the headaches which building the Castle did.*

When he began its building the 300 soldiers and marines he had been authorized to conscript from passing ships of the VOC fleet proved reluctant labourers. The official record of the stone-laying ceremony, five months after the levelling of the site had started, shows that the conscripts' share in the celebrations included 100 loaves of fresh-baked bread, eight cases of locally-brewed beer, six sheep and two oxen. It adds that the 'food and drink were delivered and placed before them, well-cooked and prepared, on the level plain of the aforesaid new fort, in the hope that these sluggish fellows by this beneficence be henceforth better encouraged and made more willing to work.' His hopes were vain. The men were poorly paid, but what little they did earn was spent in the taverns; and not until an ordinance banned the sale of drink before 6 p.m. was some sort of discipline brought to bear. Even then their approach to work was so reluctant that only a threat that future malingerers would be 'chained to their barrows' led to any real improvement.

*Yet these same walls, erected with such reluctance, house what is arguably Cape Town's finest monument to man's architectural handiwork. The Kat Balcony (**13**) which dominates the Castle's inner court is not only a splendid example of the felicitous partnership of the sculptor Anton Anreith and the architect Louis Thibault, but is a celebration of what man's labours can achieve.*

the infant shoots of the vine'). Even shy steenbok were frequently observed, though Barrow records that these, once the most numerous species in the Peninsula mountain chain, were beginning to disappear. However, perhaps its shyness, its solitary nature, has allowed even this, the largest of the Peninsula's antelope, to survive into the present – though none is as numerous as it was even 100 years ago – the urban sprawl onto the lower mountain slopes has seen to that.

Otherwise keenly observant and sensible to anything remotely scientific, 'the good Mr B.' appears to have been little interested in the wealth of creatures of the Peninsula, let alone the mountain. Even the fascinating dassie (*Procavia capensis*) drew little more comment than that its 'flesh is used for the table, but is black, dry, and of indifferent flavour'.

Had his lively interest extended to cover the mountain's fauna, his almost obsessive preoccupation with cleanliness would have warmed to the toilet habits of the steenbok who, unlike other antelope, covers his droppings with a scratching of soil. But Barrow was very much an Englishman of his time; of the many naturalists who explored the mountain his only compatriot to show a zoological flair was the redoubtable Burchell. In the scientific sphere at least, observations of the mountain's fauna seem to have been left to the Germans, Dutch and Frenchmen such as that incomparable fantasist Le Vaillant. British collectors seem to have embraced the more genteel – and, incidentally, more financially rewarding – study of the Peninsula's flora.

Non-scientific Britons on the other hand appear to have been far less pernickety – certainly prior to the first British occupation from 1795–1803. A steady stream of English visitors, such as sea captains or soldiers *en route* to India, visited the settlement in *Tafel Vallei*. The splendidly literate reprobate William Hickey called briefly in Table Bay in July 1777, a remittance man exiled by his family to India. He accompanied Colonel Gordon, the Scots 'renegade' commander of the Dutch garrison, to the Table's summit up the customary – and by now well-trodden – Platteklip route. The noble black sheep was fascinated by the antics of the dassies, amused himself and his companions by baiting scorpions, and caught a snake – described as *Copra manille* – which he preserved and proudly bore down the mountain, pickled in a bottle of gin. Not for such stalwarts as Gordon and his party the effete liquid distractions of port or madeira – their spirits demanded stronger stuff.

Perhaps the most remarkable feature of these early climbs was that the participants actually reached the mountain's top, let alone safely negotiated the descent. True, these were the times of the trenchermen, of gargantuan meals, but anyone who has scrambled up Platteklip Gorge or the even easier Kasteels Poort will attest to the foolhardiness of pausing for anything more than a snack and a few sips of water. But for their predecessors the phrase, current in the 18th century to describe the Southeaster's cloud creation, 'the tablecloth being laid' takes on a new, and literal, meaning.

Hickey's description of the mountain menus typifies the sort of meals they enjoyed:

'At eight we came to a cave or recess in the side of the huge mass of rock, forming a spacious apartment, and were very agreeably surprised at seeing a table spread with tea, coffee, cold ham, fowls, with other articles of food, all of the best kind.'

The breakfasters were serenaded from above by two military flautists whom Col. Gordon had sent on ahead of his guests and whose music persuaded Hickey 'we were suddenly got into enchanted ground, such celestial sounds burst upon our ears'. It was a nice conceit on the good Colonel's part, but unlikely to be envied by anyone who has sat on Carrells' Ledge, listening to the piet-my-vrou calling from the trees of Newlands Forest, or heard owls hooting from the star-filled sky of a Red Gods' night, or the bark of a baboon echoing across the lower table from the krantzes of Orange Kloof.

The leopards are long since gone from the Peninsula – the last recorded specimen was shot near the Round House in 1858 – but their natural prey re-

12

13

14

main. Rooting for bulbs and insects, even catching scorpions with a cautious dexterity – by raising the stone away from the body to form a protective barrier between hunter and quarry – the baboons are still plentiful in many parts of the mountain spine.

In the Cape Point Nature Reserve or squatting on the rocks of Chapmans Peak Drive, where the near-human antics of their young give the observer constant delight, baboons are as much a part of the Peninsula as the Mountain. Legend has it that they belong to two tribes, their territories divided by the no-man's-land of Noordhoek Valley, and that they never cross this boundary. But should such a division exist it is more likely to have stemmed from the road and dormitory development that flows to fill the valley as did the tides some five million years ago.

Until recently the baboons of the southern Peninsula had a reputation for aggression far greater than that of their *laissez faire* neighbours, but droughts and human expansion may have altered the temperamental balance, for there have been recent reports of hungry ones scaring Newlands forest picnickers from their rucksacks and hampers. When the Mountain larder has proved bare, baboons have always raided mountainside gardens – even brazenly entering homes under the driving pressure of hunger. Usually such forays are made by individuals, and – as the size and numbers of their troops have diminished and the farmlands and orchards shrunk – the old-time patrols by slaves to protect crops and the carbide 'guns' of pre-war years are no longer necessary. The few remaining farmers will have no regrets, but it seems a pity that today's and tomorrow's children are unlikely to see a baboon 'harvesting' a row of mealie plants: plucking an ear, tucking it under the arm, plucking another and in tucking this one away, dropping the first. . . and so on, down the row, to emerge triumphantly with one fresh ear – and a wake of wasted crop behind him.

Others of the Mountain's dwindling wild inhabitants are still driven by hunger into accessible suburban gardens. Porcupines, their flesh once prized by settlers and Hottentot alike, are seldom seen though their quills are common tokens of their passage on many of the mountain paths. Yet in a single night a porcupine can wreak havoc that even in recent years has been the despair of many a proud gardener, who can only wring his hands and notify the conservation authorities in the hopes that they will trap the culprit before further devastation takes place. When caught – and a trap baited with daffodil bulbs or apples apparently works wonders – the miscreants are transported well away from suburbia to the sanctuary of Cape Point, where by now there must be a fairly substantial population of such convicts.

However, the conservationists are not always successful. After two nights of Kalk Bay mayhem in which she had lost all her prize tulips and freesias, a well-known Cape Town actress sought help from the Department of Nature Conservation. A trap was set and baited and the third night made loud with the clamour of a caged animal, rather than fairies, at the bottom of her garden. Daylight revealed the awesome sight of her neighbours' elderly great dane wedged firmly in the trap. There was no sign of the porcupine. . .

The roar of the Cape lion will never again be heard, but for many years his cousins mourned him with nocturnal cries from the lion enclosure in the zoo on the slopes of Devil's Peak, capturing – if the night was still or the wind in the right direction – a fragment of Africa long lost to the Peninsula. And though hippopotamus no longer wallow in the marsh and reedbeds of the Amstel River, a pair introduced at Rondevlei to protect this splendid bird sanctuary from encroaching water-weed appear to be thriving – if seldom seen. Sadly, many of the Mountain's indigenous inhabitants have disappeared and others are becoming increasingly rare, but two 'foreign' creatures – the Himalayan thar and the grey squirrel – thrive so well as to pose an environmental threat.

The grey squirrel, introduced to the Peninsula from North America by Cecil Rhodes, soon established itself among the oaks and pines and spread throughout the western Cape with an enthusiasm that the empire-builder might have

16

Where other stretches of Cape Town's Atlantic coastline are endowed with sandy beaches which welcome bathers brave enough to face the water's chill, a broad seam of hard – and in places, jagged – Malmesbury Shale denies the inhabitants of Sea Point such easy access. But proximity to the city centre has ensured the suburb's continued popularity, though towering blocks of flats (15) have ousted many of the Victorian villas which nestled against the flank of Signal Hill and in the lee of the waterless heights of Lion's Head.

It is on the Sea Point front that millions of years ago the band of shale, the Peninsula's oldest geological stratum, was touched by and then mingled with the molten upswelling of the younger Cape Granite to create a natural phenomenon which is said to have made 'a major contribution to the geologists' basic conception of the relationship between sedimentary and igneous rocks'. The shale, which cleaves in even planes, thrusts above the waves of Table Bay on Robben Island and it was here that many of the flagstones for Cape Town's earliest homes were quarried. Later, salvaged, they were used in other buildings, and some form part of the floor of this domed and whitewashed Kramat (16) whose simple lines grace the slopes of Signal Hill above the city centre, and which is one of six Muslim holy places believed to protect the Peninsula from earthquakes or similar natural disasters.

17. Flanked on one side by the Twelve Apostles, the chain of mountain buttresses which Van Riebeeck named the 'Gewelbergen', and on the other by the Atlantic Ocean, the suburbs of Clifton (foreground) and Camps Bay enjoy an ever-changing seascape. Sweeping crescents of sparkling beaches are caught between rocky spits on which bungalows and other dwellings crowd; while blocks of flats hug the steeper slopes – almost to the breakers. And though the water here is colder than on the Peninsula's False Bay coast, these beaches are a year-round magnet for the young and not so young: Clifton reputedly boasts the briefest bikinis in the southern hemisphere, while Camps Bay – where gentle lawns roll to the edge of the sand – draws family picnickers on rainless days.

envied. And a pair of thars which escaped from Rhodes' Zoo found the crags of Table Mountain so to their liking that they have multiplied to the extent that their descendants threaten indigenous vegetation and must be culled. But these goat-like animals are nimble and sure-footed, keen of sight and generally inhabit the more inaccessible ledges which afford the best protection, so culling is not easy. In fact many of the most enthusiastic mountaineers have never seen a thar, though their well-worn tracks criss-cross the upper slopes and ledges and, to the inexperienced eye at least, look so like footpaths that the novice may blithely follow them. . . until confronted with an apparently unscalable rockface or yawning drop.

Since the mid-Victorian era when men and women took to the Alps in stout shoes and 'sensible' clothing and the 'sport' of mountaineering developed, Table Mountain's gage has challenged generations of climbers. At first it sufficed to find alternative routes to the top: early inhabitants of the Rondebosch-Newlands area had already explored Skeleton Gorge to the source of one of the rushing streams which still feed the Amstel, but other access – from the saddle between Devil's Peak and the main massif, up Kasteels Poort, or along the stroll from Constantia Nek to the back table – were soon blazed and established, 'as pleasurable in their various degree of exertion that the rambler and scrambler would face'.

Constantia Nek, flanked on the False Bay side by the lush vineyards of Tokai and Constantia and towards the Atlantic by the chequer-board farmsteads of the Hout Bay valley, seems especially to have caught the imagination and there are records of 'grand breakfasting after a glorious drive in a convoy of carriages' – feasts that might well have been the envy of Col. Gordon and his party – before setting off on the bridle path to. . . well, not quite to the top. The Nek had been of easy access from the earliest days of settlement and Van Riebeeck's wood-cutters had hacked out a rough track to move timber felled from the then dense indigenous forests which had given Hout Bay its name. The Nek, too, has long been a popular starting point for 'rambles and scrambles' over the Constantiaberg to the fern-dripping cavern of Elephant's Eye, which glares across the vista of the Cape Flats to the distant Hottentots Holland range, and whose vaulted chamber shows signs of man's early occupation.

Though the Peninsula's other mountains drew the sporadic attention of the early climbers – one early mountaineer boasted of having climbed each of Van Riebeeck's *Gewelbergen,* the eighteen distinctive outcrops on the Atlantic coastline today mis-named The Twelve Apostles – Table Mountain was the magnet; its vast sandstone face above the city ever its strongest pole. The bastion of the Mother City exerts a special pull, a subtle sting to which even the most hardened cannot become immune. Poised on the high pinnacle of Eagle Buttress' 'step-over route', the wide earth spread hundreds of metres beneath one's feet, or clinging limpet-like to Yellowstone Corner (the very names of the climbs have their own magic), the soul of the mountain seems to seep from the rock, permeate one's body, spreading an ichor that even time cannot erase. It is a communion of man and rock that only the mountaineer and his peers can share – beyond the imagination, perhaps, of those thousands who enjoy the ascent by cableway, opened in 1928; post cards in the special box which ensure the 'Table Mountain' franking; and admire the vista so vastly changed since De Saldanha first set foot here. A few, temporarily daring vertigo, may step to the very edge and peer at the cragsmen as they scale the 230-metre cliff of Africa Face, still the most challenging of the mountain's climbs. But the true feel of the mountain will remain beyond their reach. . .

Today's afficionados, their armoury strengthened by pitons, carabiniers and light-weight nylon ropes, still pit their skills against the rugged faces and awesome drops – new routes are opened, and overhangs which seemed impassable a few decades ago are conquered. But the mountain is a demanding god which each year claims its toll of human sacrifice – usually the careless or the tiro, but sometimes even the most experienced. It is a powerful adversary never to be challenged lightly.

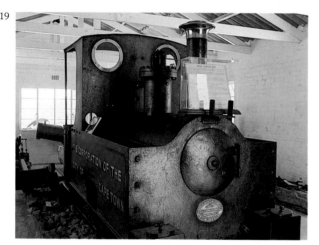

*The five-minute journey to the upper cable station (**20** and **21**) affords not only breathtaking views, but the final 100 m or so takes cable car passengers so close to the sheer sandstone that flowers and other plants are clearly visible on the narrow ledges and crevices of Africa and Arrow faces – two of the most taxing of the mountaineering routes. Antonio de Saldanha, the Portuguese mariner who made the first recorded ascent of the massif which he named Taboa do Cabo, used a site (probably near the present upper cable station) to check and correct his charts of Table and False Bays, and a large bronze relief map (**18**) similarly allows the modern visitor to 'get his bearings'. Less familiar, even to many hikers and climbers who know the mountain well, is the steam locomotive (**19**) which stands in immobile splendour on the 'back table'. The engine, which was hoisted in pieces up the mountain from Camps Bay and reassembled on the summit, operated on a single narrow-gauge line in the late 1890s, hauling the sandstone blocks used to construct reservoir walls. Its work completed, it was tumbled from its rails and left to rust. Decades later a municipal waterworks official discovered it lying hidden in a tangle of scrub; with the help of a group of enthusiasts the locomotive was refurbished, restored to working order, and given a protective roofing. Though capable of 'making steam', sadly there is nowhere for the iron horse to go.*

The match-stick cranes and derricks of Duncan Dock await the reveille of another working day (**22**). The stevedores start early and by tradition when the noon-day gun booms out its time call from Signal Hill (**23**) they down their billy-hooks and bales and turn to their 'skoff boxes' for lunch. The

22

noon-day signal, first fired in 1912, reverberates throughout the city and across Kloof Nek – a favourite starting point for ramblers (24) who enjoy the easy-going hike along the contour path with its stone-pine sentinels.

23

24

Kirstenbosch: A floral wonderland takes root

To botanists, Table Mountain is part of one of the world's great floral kingdoms – the tiniest, but its wealth of material the greatest. The mountain and its environs are home to more than 2 600 species of indigenous plants, some so limited in distribution as to be endemic to only a few square metres. But neither statistics nor science can do justice to the treasure-house of flora that comprises the *fynbos* of the western Cape. Nor does the word 'kingdom' suffice to describe its riches and the vast world of insects that live in it, for this is a wonderland empire, whose inhabitants range from the stately silver tree (*Leucadendron argenteum*) and king protea (*Protea cynaroides*) to shy, minute pelargoniums with flowers so small that one must stoop among other plants to find their hiding place.

This wealth was recognized early. Carl von Linne, the great eighteenth-century naturalist who as Linnaeus gave the world the system of classification which bears his name, described the Cape Peninsula as 'paradise on earth. . . which the Benificent Creator has enriched with his choicest wonders'. And in a letter to the then Governor of the Cape, Ryk Tulbagh (himself an enthusiastic amateur botanist), he went on to say: 'Certainly if I were at liberty to change my fortune for that of Alexander the Great, or Solomon, Croesus or Tulbagh, I should without hesitation prefer the latter.' His enthusiasm has echoed across the years and countless botanists were to visit the Cape Peninsula to examine, explore and marvel at its riches. Many still do, and Dr John Rourke of the Compton Herbarium and one of the world's leading experts on the Protea family, believes that many new species remain to be found and classified.

Long before the first settlement at the Cape, the flora of Table Mountain and its environs had captured the imagination of European naturalists, for these plants differed from those of the northern hemisphere as much as does a piece of moon rock from Malmesbury shale. Plucked by shore-line explorers or mariners stretching their sea-legs, indigenous flowers, seed-heads and even fleshy-leaved succulents were borne home to Europe as exotic mementos. Transformed by climate and the long sea voyage back to Europe, many of these were unrecognisable from their original form by the time they reached the hands of scientists; the head of a *Protea neriifolia* was so shrivelled on arrival in Amsterdam that it was classified as a thistle. Nevertheless, as such it holds the distinction of being the first of the Peninsula's plants to have its illustration published. This was in Antwerp in 1605 and Carolus Clusius's 'thistle' is a far cry from the splendid protea blooms exported throughout the world today, helping make this magnificent genus of flowering shrubs the best-known of all South Africa's plants.

Where the blou suikerbos (*Protea neriifolia*) achieved a botanic first, and the king and queen proteas – giants of the clan – still arouse international admiration, it is the less spectacular suikerbos that is perhaps dearest to the Capetonian's heart. Prolific in its nectar-rich blooms which attract hordes of delicate, long-tailed sugarbirds, it has been commemorated in countless folk-songs and, as much as the rarer red disa, must symbolize the spirit of Table Mountain. For the early settlers, too, more interested in food than botany, the suikerbos meant more than just another flower. Taking their cue from the sugarbirds, they harvested its copious nectar and as *bossiestroop* used it as a sweetener for both beverage and food. And there are still traditionalists among the folk of the Platteland who swear by its nectar as a remedy for bronchial complaints.

Though Kirstenbosch cannot encompass the full wealth of South Africa's indigenous flora, it does offer the visitor some concept of our vast range of plant life. The shyly drooping heads of a watsonia spike (**26**), the proud beak of the strelitzia, or crane flower (**27**), and the majestic thrust of the king protea, the Republic's floral emblem (**28**), provide an impressive, but miniscule, contrast. Impressive, too, are the wealth of tree fern (**29**) and cycad species that greet the walker in the gardens' 'Dell'.

26

27

28

It was the proteas that first stole, and indeed still hold, the limelight, but a plethora of other genera were soon to enchant such visiting botanists as Herrman, Masson and Thunberg – and still delight the viewer's eye. A rich range of ericas – among the most varied in size, shape and colour of all the mountain's plants – engaged the attention of Europe's gardeners in the eighteenth and nineteenth centuries. So fashionable did the cultivation of 'Cape Heaths' become, particularly in Britain, that cuttings were sold to wealthier collectors for as much as 20 guineas – a very substantial sum in those days. By 1811 no fewer than 186 species were cultivated at Kew Gardens, and of these more than half were indigenous to the Cape Peninsula and its vicinity. But the cooler northern climates were not kind to our ericas and the vogue gradually lapsed.

All are best seen on the krantzes and kloofs, plateaux and dells of their native habitat. *Disa uniflora,* the red disa or 'pride of Table Mountain' that inhabits the shaded, moss-hung banks of many of the mountain's water-courses, is an unforgettable sight. In high summer, gleaming like a red jewel, its flowering pedicels beckon the parched and weary climber with a promise of water and coolth. So synonymous are they with such promise that these blooms have given their name to the magic rills, 'disa streams', the small gulleys and courses shared with a wealth of other plants which show the gentler nature of the mountain at its best. Today, under man's encroachment, they are fewer, more remote, than was the case even a quarter of a century ago; but those who love the mountain know their secret places and it is fitting that the red disa is not only the 'official provincial flower' of the Cape, but also the emblem of the Mountain Club of South Africa.

Yet despite the city's sprawl, that has forever overlaid thousands of hectares of *fynbos,* the glories of the Peninsula's floral empire are not the preserve only of the hiker and mountaineer. Cape Town boasts one of the world's finest botanical gardens: Kirstenbosch, established in 1913 on land bequeathed to the nation by Cecil Rhodes, preserves not only plants endemic to the Peninsula and the western Cape, but much of South Africa's other indigenous flora as well. And appropriately the gardens lie just below the shadow of Van Riebeeck's Hedge, the thick boundary of wild almond which the settlement's first Commander planted to protect the VOC and free burgher herds and flocks from depredation by a Hottentot clan whose fiefdom extended over the present-day Constantia Nek and into the Hout Bay valley.

Nestling under the south-east flank of the massif and guarded by the stark sentinels of Castle and Fernwood buttresses, the cultivated section of the Gardens receive some of the highest rainfall in the Republic, with an average precipitation of 1 440 millimetres a year.

The land on which they have developed has had a chequered history. In the heyday of the Dutch East India Company one of its officials, Johannes Frederik Kusten – who for a time was secretary to Governor van Plettenberg and one of whose two wives was the widow of Martin Melck – is believed to have built a homestead there. Certainly a building of some sort existed on what is now the site of the herbarium before the second British occupation in 1806, for when the 'Kerstenbosch estate' was divided between Henry Alexander, the Colonial Secretary, and Colonel Christopher Bird, the building was renovated by Bird who used some of its Batavian tiles to build – with a delightful sense of eponymity – a bird-shaped bath around a natural spring. Today it sits at the head of what is known as 'the Dell', surrounded by one of the finest representative collections of cycads in the world.

Some years before the division of the estate, the naturalist William John Burchell remarked of it: 'Our walk conducted us to a high point of the hill of Wynberg, which overlooks Kirstenbosch, a beautiful estate belonging to the Government. The view from this spot, and indeed all the scenery around, is the most picturesque of any I have seen in the vicinity. . .'.

He had quit his post as official botanist on St Helena to spend five years exploring and recording the fauna and flora of the subcontinent and was an early protagonist of the establishment of a botanical garden in the Cape Peninsula. In his *Travels in the Interior of Southern Africa* he suggested: 'If in the vicinity of Cape Town a well-ordered botanic garden, of sufficient extent, was established for receiving plants which might casually, or even expressly, be collected in the more distant parts of the colony, the sum of money required for maintaining it would be but trifling in comparison with the advantages which science, and the public botanic gardens of England, would derive from it.'

However, Burchell's suggestion seems to have fallen on deaf ears and by the time his *Travels* was published the fun-loving Colonel Bird was firmly established on his estate with flourishing orchards and vineyards. Bird succeeded Alexander as Colonial Secretary until he quarrelled with the autocratic Governor, Lord Charles Somerset, but remained on his estate until 1843 when he returned to Europe. Burchell became a recluse and eventually committed suicide.

Rhodes added the area to his Groote Schuur estate in 1895 and had planted the magnificent avenue of Moreton Bay figs and camphor trees which bisects the lower half of today's gardens and which then formed part of a tree-lined road from Rondebosch to Constantia Nek.

After his death Kirstenbosch was neglected and became a giant sty in which literally hundreds of pigs rooted for acorns; buildings fell into ruin and the colonel's bath became overgrown and clogged with debris. It was from this unlovely wilderness that, with the political support of Sir Lionel Phillips, Professor Henry Pearson, the garden's first director, and J.W. Mathews, its first curator, began to win back the splendours that tens of thousands of visitors now enjoy each year.

One of their first undertakings was to clear Bird's bath and create the Dell. Their Augean task will be remembered with particular gratitude by a decade of University of Cape Town undergraduates. For in the late 1940s and early '50s it was something of a challenge to some of us mountain enthusiasts to leave Kirstenbosch in the early summer dawn, scramble up Skeleton Gorge, traverse the back mountain to Kasteels Poort and its descent to the Atlantic Ocean through Camp's Bay Glen. A hasty, chilly swim and the same route would be retraced until, hot and sticky, we would plunge for an illicit 'skinny-dip' in the colonel's bath – mistakenly known by many of us as 'Lady Anne Barnard's Pool'. Few, if any, had read the lively letters of Linnaeus to Tulbagh, but as we slid into the cooling balm of the waters we would have agreed with the sentiment, if not the sense, that this was one of the 'Benificent Creator's choicest wonders'.

THE TAVERN OF THE SEAS

To the early navigators it was the 'Cape of Storms', and in winter, when north-west gales whip the waters of Table Bay into a maelstrom of currents and house-high waves denying even the largest of vessels entry to the haven of the port, the name remains appropriate. These are the times when the bigger ships lay extra warps to their quayside bollards, when smaller craft drop extra anchors – sometimes in vain – at their moorings in Kalk Bay or Hout Bay, and their Coloured crewmen sip their cheap muscadel and jerepigo, glaring at the weather. The shot-heavy rains slate-shine the avenues and boulevards of the city's luxury suburbs, and scrawl their brief graffiti on the picture windows of the holiday bungalows of Melkbosstrand and Blaauwberg across the Bay.

And when the storm-tumbled sea eases and the pounding waves draw reluctantly back, it is along the strand beneath these homes that the modern beachcomber may find relics of the past. Under the lowering sky which gives the shallows a pewter hue, and tangled in the modern wrack of plastic containers, nylon ropes, boxes and bottles, may be found shards of china and delft, shell-crusted bottles – sometimes a corroded coin – bronze, silver, gold.

For these gales and rains which helped shape the land long before men first sailed the southern waters have made of the Peninsula's coast, and Table Bay particularly, a graveyard of ships. Many of these early wrecks were merchantmen, returning deep of draft and richly laden from the East and, despite the constant efforts of amateur and professional divers of today, it seems certain that treasures – artifacts if not specie – still lie shrouded by the sand and rocky outcrops beneath the turbulent waters. But the gales and powerful churning of the currents which accompany them sometimes throw up tantalising flotsam, reminders of their presence.

Not all these plump merchantmen were lost with their cargoes. In March 1647 when *Nieuwe Haerlem*, first of the VOC's ships to founder in Table Bay, ran aground off the salt pans of what is today Rietvlei, not a man was lost and the bales of oriental silks and the spices which crammed her holds were brought ashore undamaged. Even the cannons, shot and powder were landed in the ship's boats and on barges from the other vessels of the homeward-bound Dutch East India fleet. This successful salvage of *Haarlem's* cargo had a significant, if not direct, impact on the *Here XVII's* decision to establish a victualling station in *Tafel Vallei*. And one can argue that in the wreck lay the seed from which Cape Town eventually grew.

For, above all, the Dutch were businessmen. The VOC (the Dutch East India Company) had amalgamated in 1602 for the systematic commercial exploitation of the riches of the East, and its directors, the Lords Seventeen, were prepared to expend time and even lives to avoid diminution of their profits by a single stuiver. Had *Haarlem* sunk and her cargo been lost, the survivors would have found berths on the remaining ships of the fleet to return to Holland. Instead, the assistant merchant, Leendert Janszen, a far more formidable figure than his title implies, was ordered to store and protect the salvaged merchandise for shipment in the homeward fleet of the following year.

So he and his men built a fort in the dunes, which they somewhat grandiosely named 'Zandeburgh', bartered with bands of strandloping Hottentots, and hunted on the Cape Flats; they even ventured to Robben Island in search of food for the pot. Finally, 375 days after they had first come ashore and after the last of the cargo they had guarded had been loaded, they fired the hulk of *Haarlem* and sailed home with the 1648 fleet. Jan van Riebeeck was on one of those ships, and though history does not record that he came ashore, it is pleasing to imagine that he tramped the sandy walls of the first fort built on the land he would help to tame.

Janszen kept a journal of his Cape adventure, and when the establishment of a permanent station on the shores of Table Bay was mooted he was one of the men asked to draw up a report on the possibilities. He made a major contribution to what a leading historian has described as 'the first South African State paper' – the *Remonstrantie* of July 1649 – in which a fort and garden, wooden pipe-line to lead water to the beach, a jetty and even pilot boats and

32

30 *(previous page). As a south-easterly gale whips the sea to a moiling frenzy, its waves batter the breakwater of Kalk Bay harbour, dwarfing the entrance beacon and setting fishing boats a-dance at their moorings. Named for the abundance of mussel shells collected here to produce builders' lime for early Cape Town, the picturesque village was briefly the focal point of the False Bay whaling industry and, later, the Peninsula's first and most popular seaside resort.*

*Towards the end of the nineteenth century, as the Table Bay breakwater was pushed further seawards, the old double-storeyed signalling station – built in 1833 and then almost at the water's edge – was left high and dry by the harbour's spread. Relegated to a work-a-day office role, its survival was ensured by various late Victorian additions to the original structure, including the imposing clock tower (**31**) which makes the building one of Cape Town dockland's architectural gems. About the time that the clock tower was added, and with the completion of the Victoria Basin, came the introduction of the 'Penny Ferry' (**32**) which still plies across this section of the docks, saving a walk of more than a kilometre between the mole and the inner quays – separated at the basin's entrance by a mere 40 metres of water.*

34

beacons are proposed. Perhaps the most remarkable aspect of this document drawn-up for consideration by hard-headed businessmen is the humanitarianism with which it shines, particularly in the writer's attitude to the aborigines – they might, he suggests, be converted to Christianity.

However, among the *Here XVII* the realities of trade were to take precedence over lip-service to God. To them commerce and the protection of their merchandise were paramount, and never was this more apparent than in June 1773 when *De Jonge Thomas* – whose tragedy was to create South Africa's first recognized hero, Wolraad Woltemade – broke up off the Salt River mouth. No sooner had the first bales and casks of her cargo been washed ashore, and long before effective attempts were made to rescue the crew and passengers from the rapidly-disintegrating barque, a gibbet had been erected and a platoon of guards ordered to summarily hang any looter.

Woltemade, a German-born former corporal in the VOC's private 'army', was in his mid-60s at the time. His heroism went unnoticed by officialdom for more than two years and for nearly two centuries was commemorated only in the name of the Peninsula's main cemetery, the station which served it, and an uninspired piece of statuary outside the head office of an insurance company: an ironical choice in view of the long wait which the hero's widow and children faced before the *Here XVII* considered paying compensation for the loss of the family breadwinner. But then, throughout his service to the VOC, Wolraad had remained low in the Company's official pecking order.

He had for a time commanded the small outpost at Muizenberg, but by mid-1773 he was employed as a dairyman – and according to Thunberg, caretaker of the zoological gardens – a post which was something of a sinecure, a quasi pension awarded to the lower echelons of the Company's employees for faithful service. It provided a modest income, a ration allowance and a house – in Woltemade's case a long, low thatched building 'Klein Zoar' near present-day Brooklyn, which seems to have served as both dwelling and byre. From here, long before the multitude of buildings rose to chequer the littoral today, the company dairyman would have had an unrestricted view of the sweep of beach and duneland from Paarden Eiland to the very walls of the castle. And on the night of May 31 he would certainly have heard the boom of the distress cannon that signalled a shipwreck.

Such a disaster would not have been particularly novel to Woltemade. For in the twelve decades since the establishment of the settlement some 300 vessels had foundered in Table Bay, usually during winter gales. So gravely had the *Here XVII* viewed these losses that 30 years earlier they had issued instructions that between mid-May and mid-August ships were to use the alternative anchorage at Simon's Bay. But this safer winter shelter, so distant overland from the settlement's bordellos and grog-shops, was popular with neither masters nor their crews and many disregarded Amsterdam's orders. The captain of *De Jonge Thomas* was one of five who defied both the *Here XVII* and Adamastor in the winter of 1773 – and all five vessels grounded, though only *De Jonge Thomas* is remembered today, and she only because of the bravery of the soldier turned dairyman.

Riding along the beach soon after daybreak, Woltemade came upon a pitiful scene. On the farthest fringe of the breakers, pounded by heavy seas and torn by a gale which showed no sign of abating, the merchantman lay – broken in two at the mainmast and slewed broadside to the shore. Planks and spars were tumbled in the water, bales and casks tossed among the wreckage. Some of the crew clung to the mast and rails, others threw themselves into the roiling sea in what proved a vain hope of reaching the shore. The platoon of soldiers arrived from the castle to mount guard and prevent looting, for morbid onlookers had already ventured from the settlement. But Woltemade spurred his horse into the breakers, reached the ship and returned with two survivors clinging to his saddle and stirrups. Seven times he made the hazardous ride: but on the eighth, he and his horse disappeared beneath the pounding surf.

Not all the 300 or more vessels which had earlier shared the fate of *De*

33 (previous page). Containerization, the advent of mega-tankers, and the re-opening of the Suez Canal have all played a part in reducing the number of guests at the 'Tavern', while man's demand for faster communication and travel has put paid to the time-table vessels: the mailships and passenger-cargo lines which linked the Mother City to Europe, the Americas and the Far East. But there are still those who enjoy leisurely travel and Cape Town remains a popular port of call on cruise ship itineraries.

Jonge Thomas were Dutch, for although the settlement in *Tafel Vallei* was controlled by the VOC and was still essentially a victualling station for its fleets, Table Bay had become an important port of call for the ships of most other seafaring nations. French three-masters, their decks pungent with the smell of blood, would call for water and for crews to stretch their sea-legs under the tavern tables after their annual slaughter of the Cape fur seals on the rocky islands and headlands or bays of the west coast. Robben Island was no longer available to them, but there was still a rich harvest of pelts and oil beyond the narrow limits of the VOC's control. British men of war and merchantmen bound for 'John Company's' possessions in India were frequent visitors – when the two maritime nations were not at war – as were Norwegian whalermen bound for Kerguelen and what they termed the 'south ice'. Spanish and Portuguese ships, too, were frequent visitors to the Table Bay anchorage.

Their crews mixed in a veritable Babel of languages in the waterfront dives and grog-shops, where Dutch genever, the fiery arrack of the East and the equally potent 'Cape smoke' – as the local brandy was known – quenched cravings sharpened by months at sea. Doubloons, reals, shillings, sovereigns. . . all were welcome in the tills and leather pouches of the innkeepers of what was to be romantically named 'The Tavern of the Seas'. Men of many nations mingled ashore, while their ships jostled at the anchorages; and the north-west gales had no favourites when it came to destruction. Table Bay is the grave of many of their ships: in 1722, 11 British and Dutch ships went down in one night.

Not all were richly laden, and of those which were, the cargoes were sometimes saved. Yet modern divers believe that there is still treasure to be found under the centuries of silt and sand beneath the waters of the Bay. Indeed, the records bear this out. The 11 ships which sank in May 1722 included *Rotterdam* and *Zoetigheid,* carrying what was then a fortune in silver bars and Vene-

For yachtsmen the challenge of the sea remains irresistible, and the triennial Transatlantic Race from Cape Town to the South American mainland draws foreign as well as local entrants to pit their skills and strengths against the ocean's might. Spinaker set and her bows balloon-bedecked, Three Spears (34) surges away from the starting line on a day of sun and sparkling waves. But the ocean has many moods, not all of them as clement as this. Spawned by the chill Benguela current, thick fogs envelop the littoral of Table Bay with a suddenness that has taken many a mariner unawares, despite the warning beacon and the mournful claxon of the Green Point Lighthouse (35).

35

tian silver ducatoons, which were to become the objective of the first under-water salvage operation in the southern hemisphere.

Seven years before that fateful May night John Lethbridge, a Devonshire man with an inventive twist of mind, had developed what he described as a 'diving engine' with which he had had some success in recovering valuables from wrecks in the relatively shallow waters off the south coast of Britain, going down to depths of as much as 10 fathoms and remaining submerged on each dive for half an hour. When news of his successes reached Amsterdam, the *Here XVII* pricked their collective ears and decided to offer him a contract for the recovery of specie and other valuables from several accessible wrecks. In return for his services he was to receive six per cent of everything he recovered, as well as free board and lodging and a monthly salary of 110 gulden.

It cannot have been an easy or comfortable way to earn a living. The 'diving engine' was no more than a large oak barrel fitted with a glass window and waterproofed leather sleeves. There was no air hose or pump and, when submerged, the diver 'breathed the foul air' which the barrel contained and which, of course, grew increasingly foul as minutes passed underwater. At times he returned to the surface half-suffocated and on at least one occasion his face was 'blued by the asfixiation' – presumably as a result of mild carbon monoxide poisoning. Nevertheless, he was successful in recovering treasure from a Dutch East Indiaman which had sunk off Porto Santo in Madeira, and in 1727 the delighted *Here XVII* sent their valuable find – and his noisome 'engine' – to the Cape.

Their real objective was *Meresteyn,* a genuine treasure ship which had been wrecked in Saldanha Bay in 1702, but to get acclimatized Lethbridge could start on *Zoetigheid.* From her he raised 200 silver bars, each of 360 kilograms, and a considerable number of ducatoons. He also found *Meresteyn* but the currents off Jutten Island were such that his dives there failed to make any significant recovery. There is no record of their gratification but the gentlemen in Amsterdam must have been delighted by Lethbridge's efforts at the Cape where he had recovered for them some £40 000 of bullion, written off as lost, at an overall cost to the VOC of about £2 500. And there was an unexpected bonus. The diving contractor left behind one of his damaged 'engines' which two of the Company's sailors repaired and used to recover several grind-stones, twelve cannon – and several hundred ducatoons from the *Rotterdam.*

Modern divers, wearing thermal wet-suits and equipped with aqualungs, depth-gauge watches and computer-age gadgetry, which allow them much of the freedom of movement they enjoy on land, still search the Bay for treasure, though today this is more likely to be a ferro-bronze propeller or the durable cargo of a sunken steamer than ducatoons or bullion. But as they probe the sea-bed round these newer wrecks, push through the kelp-beds, stir the sand or peer through goggles at the rocky outcrops, relics of those early days of sail still come to light. Encrusted with the marine growth of centuries, old iron cannon, bullion bars, clusters of coins cemented by the ages, and even the delicate porcelains of the Orient are still to be found – many of little monetary value save to the collector, yet 'treasure' nevertheless, links in the chain which ties South Africa's mother city so securely to her seafaring past. But for the mariners of many nations, there would have been no Cape Town as we know it today; and but for the haven and watering-place which *Tafel Vallei* offered, there would have been far fewer of those early mariners.

Mariners and treasure ships. Until the middle of the eighteenth century wherever there were ocean-borne riches there were also the marine 'muggers', lurking in the sea-lanes plied by the merchantmen – and, later, slavers. These were the buccaneers, or *boucaniers* of the West Indies, better known as pirates when they operated in the waves which Britannia claimed to rule, or when their villainy took them east of the Greenwich meridian. As the maritime might of Spain declined – and with this slackened grip her pillage of the Americas – the 'gentlemen of the cutlass and the knife' sought easy plunder elsewhere. And, off the southern and east coast of Africa, they found it.

36 (previous page). Late afternoon sun bathes the beachfront cottages of Blaauwbergstrand in a mellowing light. Until recent years a sleepy hamlet of fishermen and retired city-dwellers or farmers seeking a seaside retreat, this area's commanding views of Table Bay and the mountain have attracted the developers; its character has coarsened in its new guise of dormitory 'suburb'; but after he storms that sweep its reefs and beach, relics of past shipwrecks are still to be found among the wrack.

37

The seas of the Peninsula coastline offer a wealth of activities for water-loving sportsmen. . . For the knowledgeable diver the rich harvest of crayfish or perlemoen may beckon; for the 'scuba crew' there is spearfishing or underwater exploration of wrecks. In recent years, however, surfing and sail-boarding have gained a growing following and taking a tumble (37) is part of the fun. For these surfers, pushing out through the incoming waves (38) the 'big one' is the ultimate goal. . . the chance to really 'hang ten'.

The VOC's ships, slow and cumbersome as they were, sailed in fleets on both the light outward and heavily-laden homeward voyages. Substantially armed, they numbered among their crews groups of well-disciplined and well-drilled fighting men, usually Hessians forced by economic circumstance at home to take service with the Dutch, so that – despite what one contemporary sea captain termed their 'ponderous slowness, like a gaggle of geese uncertain of the water' – they gave pause to any pirate. Stragglers might be snapped up, but they were few and far between, and *Jan Companjie* lost fewer ships or cargoes to buccaneers than to gales and faulty seamanship.

The French and their English arch-rivals in India appear to have been the main targets for the pirates who lurked in the well-frequented channel between Madagascar and the mainland and made their lairs on the smaller islands – Reunion, Seychelles and the Comoros. Usually they left the Cape, with its fort and substantial garrison, well alone, though several, including the notorious Captain Kidd, called here for water and supplies. But the VOC did not sail unscathed. In 1720 a pirate fleet led by John Plantain and the French buccaneer Jean de la Bouche completed a profitable cruise and sold their loot to the Company representatives in Cochin – and then attacked Dutch merchantmen carrying these same spoils back to Holland.

Quarter was seldom given or expected, and there was little honour among the seafaring thieves. However, Table Bay was the setting for one of the most treacherous acts of duplicity committed, not by the pirates but by the British authorities. In the early 1700s, in an attempt to sweep the oceans clean, the Admiralty sent out a force of three powerful warships under a Commander Warren to wipe out the pirates' nest on St Mary's Island off the east coast of Madagascar. This was a robbers' roost in the finest story-book tradition, its sparkling sandy beaches fringed with palms and centred on a lagoon, ideal for careening the pirate ships and also easily protected. It was this that defeated Warren's expedition. Warned of the warships' approach, the pirates sank two of their own craft, effectively blocking the entrances to the harbour lagoon, and manned the fort they had built to command it.

The stalemate was broken by Warren's offer of a free pardon to any of the buccaneers who would foreswear piracy, and a promise to let them retain their loot. Most accepted this chance of what would amount to wealthy respectability, and an American sea captain, Samuel Burgess, offered them a passage to America. On the voyage Burgess put in to Table Bay for supplies and fresh water, and during his short stay an armed East Indiaman, *Loyal Merchant* – which had a royal commission to seize any pirates – also put in to port. In spite of the Governor's protests and Warren's promise of a pardon, Burgess's ship was seized, along with its passengers and their loot, and sailed to India where the reformed pirates were tried and most were hanged. . . their brief spell of honesty having failed to prove the best policy.

But though the seas surrounding the Peninsula's coastline have swallowed man's ships and treasure, they have given up many treasures of their own. From the earliest times there was an abundance of marine food. The numerous strandloper middens along the shore offer evidence that for at least part of each year the earliest inhabitants of the Peninsula subsisted on a largely shellfish diet. As they developed their skills they made stone fish traps – rocky pools covered at high tide from which any fish that ventured in could not escape when the water receded. The tidal swimming pool at Dalebrook was constructed on the site of one of these traps, and along the coast beyond Arniston a string of them remains, still used by the local fishing community at Skipskop. And of course for several decades before the establishment of Van Riebeeck's tiny settlement, whalermen and sealers had harvested these seas and shores.

Today, perhaps too late, we have begun to realize that man's plunder of the sea must be controlled; but to the early seafarers and settlers its resources must have seemed limitless, though they made remarkably little use of them from an economic point of view. From the earliest days the Portuguese had fished the rich Aghulas Bank – several of Vasco de Gama's crew became seriously ill

38 ▶

after eating fish caught at Mossel Bay – and the then abundant schools of snoek, kabeljou and haarder in the waters of Table Bay provided much of the protein for Van Riebeeck's garrison: so much so that there was a suggestion of munity, with irate soldiers demanding an increase in their rations of beef or pork. But such protests fell on deaf ears and 'to show that we will not submit to orders from the herd' the doughty Governor increased the frequency of fish on the daily menu, and to stress his displeasure added penguin flesh and other seabirds to the cookpots of the fort.

Fish were caught with handlines to feed the early settlement and later the growing slave population, but the establishment of the victualling station in *Tafel Vallei* brought welcome relief for passing mariners from the salted fish diet: they now revictualled their vessels with sheep and cattle, so that in a sense – and for a while at least – fishing of the Peninsula's waters actually declined. Such fish as were caught were named for their similarity to those known in Holland. What they will have made of the *blaasop*, or evil-eyed puffer, is not recorded, though the German astronomer Peter Kolbe, who arrived at the Cape in 1705, described it as well as 24 other Cape species of fish and marine life in his book published in 1719.

The indigenous inhabitants had probably warned the settlers of the toxic properties of this fish, for there is no record of early deaths from such poisoning. However, a group of redcoats died after a 'fry-up' of *blaasop* caught at Muizenberg during the first British occupation of the Cape, and a sailor on a French corvette which visited Simon's Town in the 1840s, suffered a similar fate after sampling what he obviously considered to be a new culinary delicacy. In fact these fish – there are some 24 species in South African waters, where they are the bane of anglers – proved so much of a hazard that until recently the British Admiralty's *Africa Pilot Part II* carried the following dire description: 'There is a fish in Simon's Bay commonly called toad-fish, about six inches long; back dark, with deep black stripes; belly white, with faint yellow patches. It swims near the surface, and is a constant attendant on lines employed fishing. When taken from the water it puffs out considerably. Should any portion of the fish be eaten, death ensues in a few minutes.'

Though fishing had little economic significance in the first decades of the settlement at the Cape, Van Riebeeck did exploit other marine resources of the coast. His hopes of establishing a whaling station were not to materialize, but sealing made an important contribution to the economic viability of his outpost and tens of thousands of pelts – those of the bulls are known as 'wigs' – were shipped to Holland, while seal oil was exported to Batavia, as well as being used for almost a century as the main source of illumination at the Cape. Even this substantial slaughter seems to have had little impact on the seal population, and when Simon van der Stel visited False Bay in 1688 – 'to see whether . . . might not be discovered a well-situated "hoek" with an abundance of fish so that the inhabitants and the Company's slaves might be more abundantly provided with fresh and salted fish' – he sailed to Seal Island.

He sent men armed with clubs ashore and recorded: 'They could on landing find no spot on which to place their feet without treading on seals or birds, which had no means of defending themselves when being killed except with their beaks and wings. The seals rushed with such multitudes into the sea that the boat on her approach could hardly float.'

With his party he sailed back to Kalk Bay where a lion made off that night with one of their sheep, so that Nature took some slight retribution for the day's slaughter.

Kalk Bay, today a charming little fishing harbour and mini-colony for artists, was uninhabited at the time of Van der Stel's expedition to False Bay, though caves on the steep flanks of Trappies Kop, which protects the bay from the south, had been home to Middle and Late Stone Age man. The largest, Neptune's Cave, was occupied by a small group of strandlopers for much of the year, though they were apparently away during the ten days when the Governor and his men camped above the beach, where there was abundant fire-

46

39. *From the sylvan tumble of the Glen, a popular picnic area stretching from Kloof Nek to the upper limits of suburban Bakoven and Camps Bay, the full sweep of the Twelve Apostles – capped here with South-easter cloud – is seen to best advantage. The Glen, too, is the site of the Roundhouse, once a hunting lodge favoured by Sir Charles Somerset and today a popular restaurant.*

40

42

48

wood and a perennial stream provided clear fresh water. Neptune's Cave, incidentally, can probably lay claim to having been the longest, almost continuous human habitation in the Peninsula. Not only did Stone Age people and, later, strandlopers enjoy its shelter and the vista it affords, but in recent years it has been the home of successive families of Coloured fishermen.

When I climbed Trappies Kop early in 1980, I found a large iron double bedstead, complete with a mattress and blankets, dominating the cave. There were stone and driftwood shelves and the floor, neatly swept with a brushwood *besem*, had been marked off into rooms with rows of stones. There was even an old dustbin outside the 'front door' – the inhabitants of today being more conscious of tidiness than the midden-makers – and the occupant told me that he and his family had lived there for several years, though it was *'darem 'n bietjie koud in winter'*!

A small military garrison was stationed at Kalk Bay from 1795 onwards, partly to protect travellers on the overland route to Simon's Bay and partly to contain the Bushman and Hottentot clans which still roved the Peninsula south of Noordhoek valley. For a brief spell from 1806-11 it was the centre of a busy whaling industry in False Bay, where for centuries huge schools of baleen whales had come to calve. A large, corroded ring sunk in the flat rocks near the present Wiley's Pool – where the whales were hauled ashore for flensing when the tide receded – and several cauldrons in which the blubber was reduced and which now grace the lawns of Seaforth beach, are the only mementos of that period when a cry of 'Thar she blows' or *'Halva-blast'* would send the shore-based whalermen scurrying for their harpoons and longboats.

But the carnage of those years made the whales wary of their once-popular calving grounds and they returned in such diminishing numbers that whaling in False Bay ceased to be profitable. Sporadically a few still return to calve off Fish Hoek beach and delight the Christmas-time holiday visitor, but never again are the inhabitants of the False Bay coast likely to see the dark, humped backs of these leviathans in their hundreds, the spume from their vent-holes turning the surface of the bay to a very Tivoli of fountains.

Whales were no strangers to Table Bay either, but, though a little whaling was carried out, it was not until 1789 that a whale fishery was established and Van Riebeeck's dream of a full-scale operation to harvest the mammals was realized. Two years later Messrs Fehrsen formed a company which controlled whaling in the bay and along the coast, rendering down the blubber for oil and preserving the baleen – vital in making the fashionable stays and corsets of the day. But shipping the oil was costly and the Fehrsens do not seem to have been particularly disappointed when in 1803 the Batavian Republic granted a concession for the sole rights to whaling in Table Bay to the South African Chartered Fishing Company. Some indication of the Fehrsens' success – or lack of it – can be gained from the fact that they were given 23 slaves as the only compensation for the loss of their whaling interests.

South Africa no longer participates in whaling – the shore-based station at Donkergat near Saldanha closed in 1967 and that at Durban in 1979 – but the Tavern of the Seas was until recently the final staging post for the world's whaling fleets, as the giant factory ships and their flotillas of high-bowed catchers headed for the whaling grounds on the fringes of the 'south ice'. Lawrence Green has recalled his boyhood memories of the old Nantucket whalers: 'They were the square-rigged "spouters" out of Nantucket and New Bedford, sails darkened by blubber smoke, stumpy masts and swift boats at the davits. . . a sight that draws men and women away from well-laid tables as the black fleet steams along the waterfront against the golden sunset.'

And I remember in the early 1950s visiting Russian and Scandinavian catchers, crossing precarious planks to reach snug quarters where one drowned the smell of bilges and oil with the glasses of vodka or aquavit that bridged the language barrier. The crews were rough, roistering, bearlike men – but friendly and hospitable to a young journalist besotted by the call of the sea. The break in diplomatic relations with the Russians put paid to the evenings of vodka and

Visiting in the 1850s, a Victorian said of the Peninsula's Atlantic coastline: 'As a chamaeleon changes his colours, so does this sea-girt stretch change textures. Smooth strand, steep crag and water-worn boulders all vie with the tides in a walk of less than an hour. . .' The same is true today, so that a family group can find mid-day breathing space on the rocks at Oude Kraal (40) as easily as the early morning stroller on the beaches at Clifton (41), though later in the day these same sandy coves are thronged (42) with those who do not mind having to share the sea and sun.

caviare, and the world's whaling fleets have shrunk as our awareness of a need to conserve the great leviathans of the oceans has expanded. No more do they visit the Tavern of the Seas.

Fishing on an industrial scale is a comparatively recent development in South African waters, and again an awareness of dwindling resources – over-catching for several years shocked even the most commercially greedy when they viewed the resultant diminishing harvest – has led to restrictions and the imposition of quotas, particularly for pelagic fish, and that delight of all lovers of seafood, the Cape rock lobster or *kreef.*

Fishing for local consumption, mainly with handlines, became largely the province of Cape Malays and Coloureds who used to put out in small boats from Rogge Bay almost daily except at the height of the winter storms. Delightful paintings and sketches of the early days of the young town show these fishermen – or their womenfolk – hawking their catch through the streets.

More than 30 years separated their activities, but it took a down-to-earth German and the *joie de vivre* of a Frenchman – one with an eye to the commercial possibilities of dried salt fish, the other with a gourmet's appreciation of rock lobster – to effectively father South Africa's fishing industry. In doing so, they changed the face of Hout Bay.

In 1867 Jacob Trautmann, an immigrant farmer in the Hout Bay valley, decided that the shoals of snoek which teem off the Peninsula's Atlantic coastline in autumn and early winter could be harvested, salted and dried – a process which his Baltic ancestors had perfected generations previously. The snoek – a large mackerel-like fish with a powerful predatory jaw – tends to deteriorate more quickly than the European species with which Trautmann was familiar; but he devised a way of preserving it and found a ready market for the product among the protein-hungry workers of the sugar plantations of Mauritius. And an export industry was born which a century later was to put South Africa briefly in the 'Top Ten' of the world's fishing nations.

Snoek are still landed and processed at Hout Bay, although smoking has replaced Trautmann's methods, and are now a favoured delicacy rather than a labourer's diet; and today the fishing fleet also catches rock lobster. Some still remember when this, too, was part of the working man's daily fare and a large bag of the succulent claws and legs could be bought for a penny.

Here it was the Frenchman Lucien Plessis who realized the full potential. In 1903 he bought the hull of a British barque, *R. Morrow*, which had been wrecked off Mouille Point. He had it towed to Hout Bay and turned it into a canning factory to process rock lobster which he exported to France. A mysterious explosion in 1914 tore the factory apart, killing M. Plessis and seven of his employees. But the fish-canning industry which he began still flourishes, and rock lobster tails processed at Hout Bay are now an international export.

Few Capetonians can afford crayfish today; reduced quotas have made them a rare delicacy unless there is a skindiver in one's family. Inspectors keep constant watch to see that no one exceeds his daily quota of five crayfish – which must be over a certain size and may not be in berry – though there are still places where with a nod and a wink, the right introduction, and at a price not too unreasonable in these days of inflation, one will find a parcel of *kreef* in the back of his car.

But for the hand-line fishermen of Hout Bay and Kalk Bay the snoek of all marine creatures is of paramount importance, the economic backbone of their existence. To those of Kalk Bay, particularly, a good snoek season means rejoicing: if the runs are poor, belts have to be tightened. Mainly owned by the Coloured fishermen themselves and manned by descendants of families who have fished together for longer than their memories serve, the small boats put out in the dark of early morning and usually return about noon. If the catch has been good a skein of seagulls will trail behind the boat in an avian riband of success, dropping in twos or threes to squabble over offal which the crew discard as they clean and salt the best of the day's harvest for home use.

The quayside is abustle with fishmongers and onlookers, and as the boats

Beer, though vastly different from that canned or bottled today, was one of the earliest beverages brewed at the Cape where – despite inroads made by wine in recent years – its popularity remains unchallenged. In common with their fellow South Africans, many Capetonians argue that beer is indispensable to any braai, whether held on the lawns above Camps Bay beach (43), at other popular picnic spots, or even in the privacy of a garden. . . for it is versatile: lager can be used to baste the meat or sausage; it is an effective dowser of unruly flames that threaten to scorch the tjops; and of course it can be drunk – preferably copiously and while someone else prepares the fire or turns the wors. Many of the Mother City's sons have stomachs which bear silent, or rumbling, testimony to their dedication to this supervisory art. . .

43

follow one another to unload the fish and the gleaming catch is thrown ashore, the bargaining and bidding begin. Traditionally the entire catch goes to one buyer, though when the sea has been particularly bountiful – and a catch of a thousand or more snoek by one boat is not unknown – a syndicate may quickly form to buy the whole lot. By tradition, too, bids are made for the price of one fish which then goes for the entire catch, be it 30 or 300. And the bids are still made in shillings and pence (though today more frequently in pounds and shillings) – for these conservative fisherman have no truck with the niceties of decimalized coinage! So the calls come: 'Seven en six. . . seven en eleven. . . eight bob. . .' until a mutually satisfactory price is reached – often hastened by the skipper's knowledge that the vessel about to round the breakwater into the tiny harbour has a larger catch which may soon deflate prices.

For many years, and even into the immediate post-war period, fishmongers and hawkers would load their purchases into horse-drawn carts, keeping the fish cool and moist under wet sacking or even Port Jackson willow branches, and race along the main road past St James and Muizenberg to reach their ready markets in Steenberg, Retreat, the *Vrygrond*, and even the farmsteads of Constantia and Tokai, where the first fingers of suburban development were feeling out to replace the vines with villas. Then, long before you heard the castanets of his horse's hooves or the squeaky grumble of his iron-rimmed cartwheels, the mournful call of the fish horn would herald the hawker's approach. Today the fishmongers come in bakkies, the fish loaded into plastic containers lined with ice: there are few fish carts and the bray of the short tin horn is seldom heard on the streets of the suburbs.

Caught from September to July, with the season and fish at their best between October and January when the vast silver shoals arrive in False Bay, the snoek are becoming less predictable in their movements and some marine scientists believe that their numbers may be diminishing. Should this prove so, the Kalk Bay fishermen, already dwindling in numbers, may soon disappear, seeking jobs in factories or on the land, and taking with them yet another facet of colourful history and tradition.

. . .But when the last of the braaivleis embers have been scuffed out with sand or drowned with sea water – lager is for less utilitarian libations – and the last of the beer cans kicked into untidy piles, and the kids and the grids and the cool-bags bundled into the car, a quiet descends on Camps Bay. As the clouds build up on the horizon and the sun dabs the first touches of its afterglow across the scene (44), the smell of ozone, the iodine of kelp, replace the aroma of melting mutton fat, and peace returns to the coast.

Hout Bay, so named for the indigenous forests of its valleys which filled much of the early settlers' need for timber, has not escaped the growing city's grasping demand for space, the Midas fingers of the developers. Yet it manages to retain a rural charm. There are farmlands here, and orchards, space still for paddocks and horses which can be exercised on the firm beach sand below the Sentinel (46) as the incoming tide wipes out the prints of hooves or the tracks of a lolloping dog. In early days the bay was reached only by sea or the rough track which the woodcutters had hewn across Constantia Nek. Now it is more accessible, served by several roads, including the scenic, cliff-hugging Chapmans Peak drive (45) cut from the living rock and said to equal the French corniche in its spectacular views.

Indeed some of their traditions have already felt the first nibble of erosion, not as a result of the sea's depletion, but from man's ignorance and greed.

Until recently a quayside service was held annually in late April or early May to bless the fleet, see the crews safely through the year ahead, and ensure good catches. It was an ecumenical service which embraced a cross-section of religions to which Kalk Bay's fishermen belong. In their full regalia of vestments and accompanied by surpliced choristers, the Anglican rector of Kalk Bay's charming thatched Holy Trinity Church, the Catholic priest from the church of St James, which has given its name to Cape Town's smallest suburb, and the local Imam would combine in a service of joy, hope and thanksgiving. But a dictum by the Ayatollah Khomeni that Muslims should not mix in worship with people of other faiths led in 1981 to the withdrawal of the Imam from the ceremony; and to yet another crack in the wall of Kalk Bay's long tradition of comfortable co-existence.

Table Bay, too, is the home of a fishing fleet, but mainly of trawlers whose men lack the community of character of the fisherfolk of Hout Bay and Kalk Bay. These country cousins sometimes follow the fish round the Peninsula and into its northern waters but there is little love lost between the trawlermen and the line fishermen, and they keep to themselves, even while sharing the Alfred Basin – South Africa's first true dock.

Today this is virtually a miniscule backwater, lost in the 280 hectares which, with the container berths and Duncan Dock, comprise Cape Town's port complex. But when it was completed and officially opened by Prince Alfred, Queen Victoria's second son, the 3,5 hectares of water which the basin encompassed provided the first real measure of winter safety for ships in Table Bay. The VOC's orders about wintering in Simon's Bay had so long been disregarded as to be forgotten, and since the second British occupation the toll of marine losses to the northeast gales had read like a Lloyd's underwriter's nightmare. In the great gale of May 1865 alone 16 ships were wrecked, including the steamer *Athens,* and 60 lives were lost.

The first mariners to use Table Bay as a harbour anchored a kilometre or more off-shore, transporting their goods, chattels and themselves across the choppy waters and through the breakers in lighters. This final stage, among the curling surf, was usually spray-damp and the hazards of capsizing were always present: womenfolk and dignitaries were often borne through the shallows to dry ground, pick-a-back or on the boatmen's shoulders. To reduce both risk and discomfort work began in 1656 on a wooden jetty near the present site of the Castle and when completed two years later 'allowed of landing with greater comfort and facility'.

Nothing more was done to improve the harbour as such until the garrison and their lords in Holland were shocked into action by the loss of nine ships and cargo valued at £160 000 in a single May gale in 1737. The fact that 200 lives were lost will also have caused at least some concern: and the disaster spurred their decision to build a breakwater in whose lee anchored vessels would gain some protection from the high, gale-swept sea of winter. And the Council of Policy laid down that every farmer bringing a load of produce to market in the settlement should then use his wagon to cart a load of stone to Mouille Point where work on the breakwater started.

Well aware of the massive force that combined wind and wave could exert, the local planners stipulated that the mole should be 30 metres wide at the base, tapering to an eight-metre peak – an engineering project of no mean scope even by today's standards and one which even the most optimistic of the Council of Policy's members must have realized would take mind-boggling numbers of wagon-loads to achieve. And the agricultural growth of the relatively tiny hinterland is shown both by the fact that the work progressed at all and that by 1745 the breakwater had been pushed 320 metres into the sea. When one remembers the relatively primitive character not only of the technique but of the equipment, this slow seaward crawl – at a rate of some 40 metres a year – of tonne after tonne of rock and quarried stone was a remarka-

When the snoek are running well, there is joy in the fishermen's cottages and flats of Kalk Bay, on the False Bay coast, and in Hout Bay across the narrow Peninsula. Catches are hurled casually onto the quayside (47) in anticipation of buyers' bidding that will be brisk. But there are times, maybe with shoals close to shore, when gales confine even the larger boats to port, and oilskinned fishermen (48) must wait anxiously for a change in the wind.

ble achievement. The fierce currents which sweep that stretch of coast shifted the fill almost as quickly as the wagons could dump it, and the winter storms bit hungrily at the completed section; yet still the spans of oxen hauled and the breakwater grew.

But where the forces of the sea could not halt its progress, a tiny creature – or a myriad of them – could. Like some biblical scourge, a swarm of locusts enveloped the farms of the Boland; fields and orchards were stripped; and with no produce for the farmers to bring to town, their wagons could not be compulsorily inspanned to haul stone. Agricultural recovery was slow, and the set-back seems to have taken all the steam out of the breakwater project. Work became desultory, then ceased altogether. Today, when tides are particularly low, man's first attempt at training the South Atlantic shows its remains, encrusted by more than two centuries of marine growth.

Almost a century was to pass before the Tavern of the Seas was made more hospitable to winter visitors – as far as vessels were concerned. For their crews it had long been a different matter – the waning of the VOC's power and the resultant growth of free enterprise had seen to that. Even before the first occupation by Britain, whose ports had long enjoyed a reputation for their cathouses and grog shops – which, incidentally, were also invaluable 'recruiting offices' for the press gangs – the waterfront saloons and bordellos of Table Bay had an unsavoury popularity among the world's mariners. And though the rigid Calvinism of the settlement's burghers led to occasional forays by the town guards or *Ratelwag* into the seamier waterfront dives, madams such as the notorious 'Hottentot Nell' and 'Portuguese Rosie' operated their 'stables' with relative impunity.

The British occupations, firstly in 1795 and finally in 1806, saw a tremendous increase in trade with the Cape and, consequently, a boom in maritime visitors, both ships and seamen. There was a corresponding boom in equally commercial but perhaps less worthy spheres, and the Tavern drew this self-righteous comment from one contemporary: 'For licentiousness and sottery, this place has no equal in the southern hemisphere, save perhaps Valparaiso. . . whores and drunks abound'. The writer, a parson *en route* to the East, was probably laying it on a bit thick for Cape Town's low-life was certainly no worse than that of any other port of the time and, given its relatively small permanent population, possibly more decorous than most.

But if the advent of British administration led to a more generous, even permissive, hospitality for the seafarers of the world, it did nothing to protect their ships – or, at least, not until another great gale forced the new authorities to action. In 1831 six vessels sank, taking with them cargo then valued at £50 000 to the bottom of the Bay. Much of the earlier breakwater had disappeared and instead of resurrecting this project it was decided to extend a stone pier from the foot of Bree Street. This would be used in winter to provide vessels with extra cables and even anchors, and the work would be financed from charges levied on cargoes loaded from or landed on the jetty. The concept of a sturdy pier was welcomed, but that of a levy was not. A storm of protest from the recently-established Legislative Council beat about the ears, not only of Sir Benjamin d'Urban the Governor, but of the authorities in Whitehall, for the bulk of the Council's members were merchants, no less jealous of their profits than the *Here XVII* had been, and even more reluctant than the gentlemen in Amsterdam had been to pay for an elaborate construction in stone when a substantial but cheaper jetty could be built from wood.

Commerce rather than compromise appears to have won the day, and work began on sinking wooden piles stretching out from the shore near the Castle; and also on a second jetty – this of stone – but that progressed far more slowly. However, it came into use in 1842: the merchants, like today's entrepreneurs, discovered ways of passing on the levy to the consumer without affecting turnover or profits; and when, six years later, work was started on a second pier – at the foot of what was soon to be renamed Adderley Street – Cape Town's tradesmen no doubt puffed contentedly on their pipes and cigars, swallowed their port, and reflected that all was for the best in the best of all possible worlds. And indeed records from that period show that they had reason for satisfaction: business was booming, with a constant to-ing and fro-ing from the piers and jetty of barrels and bales as varied in size as in content.

And for the next nine decades the jetty at the foot of Adderley Street was to accommodate a range of 'entertainments' as bizarre as the diversity of the cargoes landed on its mighty teak decking. As well as playing its commercial role, it fulfilled all the functions of its counterpart at a European resort: there were

48

49. *Under a pewter sky heavy with its promise of storm, the waters of the Atlantic surge from their long unbroken course to beat on the rocky stretch of coastline between Hout Bay and the sweeping spread of sands that marks the opening of the Noordhoek valley to the south.*

'freak' shows, pierrot troupes, angling contests, and much more. At the turn of the last century a large rotunda at its shoreward end was the permanent home of Fillis's Circus, housing not only the Big Top but the customary menagerie – including five Indian elephants which were led weekly across the sand and shingle to bathe in the waters of the Bay. Later there was a snake-park, and between the two World Wars the Cape Town Symphony Orchestra – much smaller then than now – gave promenade concerts on Sunday afternoons. I have a somewhat distant memory of one such concert, preceded by a visit to the snake-park: a sparkling day alive with sound and colour as only those of early childhood can be; the sun glinting on the keys of Reggie Clay's flute; and though I cared not at all for the snakes, I did enjoy the music. And there was a pirate who sold ice-cream. He was said to have been wounded somewhere in Flanders, but he must have been a pirate – how else explain his wooden leg and crutch and black eye-patch?

The Pier has gone now, swallowed by the amorphous reclaimed mass of the Foreshore. A large hotel towers where Fillis's elephants once bathed, lounge lizards have replaced the snakes, and a cacophony of cars dispels the shades of past musicians. But descendants of the seagulls that strutted and quarrelled on the Pier continue the feud today.

Among some Pacific island tribes the seagull is believed to represent the souls of drowned sailors; distorted by the wind, its cry can sound remarkably like human anguish. But when the pounding waves explode their spray high above the breakwater, and the mewling of the Cape gulls sheltering in whatever lee they can find, is shredded by the wind, the tatters of their cry echo those of early sailormen and of convicts too. For the old breakwater was built by such men, and its stones, encrusted with the sea's salt, have known the sweat and tears of five decades of prisoners. The breakwater and a chill grey building fronting Portswood Road are silent memorials of one of the more shameful episodes in Table Bay's varied history.

The powerful commercial faction in the Legislative Council was satisfied with the facilities afforded by the wood and stone 'piers', but not the authorities; for while the jetties made cargo handling easier and greatly reduced the risk of salt-water damage to the merchants' bales, they afforded little real safety to the ships which carried those cargoes. A breakwater, protecting two harbour basins deep enough for ships to tie up alongside the quays, would provide the solution and meet everyone's needs. But the cost of the first plan, drawn up in 1857, was a prohibitive £1 million. This time not only members of the Legislative Council and the powerful Commercial Exhange demurred, but Whitehall – in the person of William Gladstone, then Britain's Chancellor of the Exchequer – viewed the cost with equal alarm. Had the proposal come hard on the heels of a major shipping disaster, Whitehall and even the burghers might have felt differently but – at least as far as Table Bay was concerned – the Lutine Bell at Lloyds had tolled for a vessel lost here with unprecedented infrequency for the past decade. So instead a compromise, cut-price proposal was accepted. A shorter breakwater and smaller basins would be built and, using convict labour, the cost of the project would not exceed £400 000. Thus the notorious Breakwater Prison came into being.

Were its results less sorry, less bestial, the typical touch of mid-Victorian hypocrisy in this decision would be laughable, coming as it did from Gladstone, that 'most liberal and humane of British statesmen', and endorsed as it was by the very pillars of Cape Town society who less than a decade previously had so vociferously condemned 'the introduction and employment of convicts anywhere in the Colony'.

It could be argued that their earlier opposition was to 'immigrant' convicts, while those whose money-saving labour they so willingly endorsed were home-grown, but this is mere hair-splitting: the dehumanizing effect of the contemporary penal system was the same, whether the sentence was imposed for the theft of a loaf of bread in Britain in the late 1840s or for I.D.B. in Kimberley 20 years later.

But the self-righteousness of Capetonians had known no bounds when, in 1849, they learned that despite earlier protests to the Governor and the British Government, *HMS Neptune* was on her way to the Colony with 282 convicts destined to serve their sentences not in Australia, where gaols were already bursting at the bars, but at the Cape. By the time she dropped anchor in Simon's Bay on September 19 several members of the Legislative Council had resigned; others appointed in their stead had, after nearly being lynched, followed suit; and there were dire threats that anyone who had dealings with the ship would be boycotted. Out of sight, in this instance, was not out of mind.

An even greater furore of protest erupting into riots and demonstrations brought the everyday life of the town to a standstill and, according to a contemporary report, 'so little work or business was done that every day seemed like a Sunday'. There could scarcely have been more brouhaha if *Neptune*

50

When winter gales lash the Cape of Storms, they are at their most furious in Table Bay, and it was with this in mind that the VOC decreed that its fleets should use Simon's Bay on the False Bay coast as a winter anchorage. Though many captains ignored the order – daunted by the overland journey they and their crews would face to reach the settlement – a harbour grew and with it the dockyard port of Simon's Town, where first the Royal Navy and later the South African Navy thronged the winding streets, paraded (51) down its central thoroughfare and packed the taverns where their crests and badges are displayed (52). Even during the South-easters of summer Simon's Bay offers shelter, while St James (50) reputedly shares with adjacent Kalk Bay the most windless and clement of all the Peninsula's weather; yet Fish Hoek – only a few kilometres distant – bears heavy brunt of both winter and summer winds.

had anchored in Table Bay and her cargo of felons brought ashore and given the freedom of the city. In fact, many of the convicts chained below decks were not criminals in the accepted sense of the word but Irish patriots who had been on the fringes of the ill-fated uprising against British rule in the previous year, and many of the colonists – as much prisoners of British colonial policy as the 'gaol-birds' anchored off Simon's Town – may have shared their political sympathies. But the issue had become so emotionally intense that there was no room for logic. A Bowler painting of the scene outside the Commercial Exchange when more than 5 000 met in protest captures the furious atmosphere. Top-hatted figures gesticulate, and even the clouds look angry.

For more than five months, while orders, proposals and counter-proposals passed between the Cape and Whitehall, *Neptune* lay at anchor in Simon's Bay. Spring turned to blazing summer and the heat below decks must have made the prospect of a penal colony seem almost Utopian to the men in chains. Nor can the enforced stay have given much pleasure to her crew. A handful of bold entrepreneurs had broken the boycott, but the provisions they were able to supply were meagre, and shore-leaves were hardly more congenial than conditions on board. Sailors were mocked, refused service in the taverns and sometimes attacked by the angry populace. Even local ladies of easy virtue, the whores, affected by public sentiment, ostracised the crew.

In Britain, Charles Bowyer Adderley made impassioned speeches in Parliament on behalf of the colonists' cause, earning himself such gratitude from the citizens of Cape Town that they gave his name to the Heerengracht and voted him a magnaminous £100 from public funds. To what extent his efforts influenced the final decision on the convicts' fate is uncertain; probably the fact that the Governor, Sir Harry Smith, sympathised with the Capetonians had a more telling effect. But on February 21, 1850, to the relief of convicts and crew as much as of the Capetonians, *Neptune* sailed for Australia.

To the historian, her visit and long and stormy stay has a significance out of all proportion to the actual event, for it was the first time that colonists anywhere in the Empire had forced the British Government to reverse a decision, other than through open rebellion or by going to war. But to the socio-moralist, the demonstrations and protest meetings seem shabby piety in the light of the complacency with which a decade later the same civic leaders accepted the convicts of the Breakwater Prison, right on their own doorstep. At its most crowded the forbidding gaol in Portswood Road housed more than 1 000 convicts, and the dreadful conditions under which they worked and existed, combined with the brutality of some of the warders, earned it a reputation as grim as that of the French penal colony of Devil's Island. The only touch of graciousness about the entire project was perhaps the silver trigger which Prince Alfred, then Duke of Edinburgh, squeezed to tip the first truck-load of stone into Table Bay to initiate construction of the breakwater.

Progress fluctuated. A gale which blew continuously for 17 days in the winter of 1882 wreaked so much damage to the mole that the authorities seriously considered abandoning the scheme. And in May three years later, when 18 ships were wrecked and 60 lives lost, the construction engineers estimated that some 60 000 tonnes of stone had been shifted by the waves. Yet in spite of this set-back the uncompleted mole had proved its value, for the ships at the jetties in the breakwater's lee were unscathed by the storm. And of course progress also hinged on the number of convicts available to quarry the stone and then, leg-irons clanking, move it. As late as 1895 a local commentator was to write: 'The breakwater depends entirely for its rate of progress on the output of I.D.B. convicts from Kimberley' — obviously referring to the output of the courts, rather than that of the prisoners.

In the late 1940s, though the prison as such had closed 30 years before, the buildings retained a chill forbidding atmosphere. It was as if the anguish and despair of all those thousands of men and women who had been confined there had seeped into the very stones and mortar, never to be eradicated. And the walls showed evidence of the prisoners' presence. Among the graffiti in the solitary-confinement cells of the punishment block one stood out in impeccable copper-plate: 'Three days cells for two big smokes — it won't break my heart', was its laconic message, so different from the embittered scrawls and scratchings which surrounded it, and not least in its penmanship — a reminder that not only hardened felons laboured in the quarries and on the mole.

Many of the inmates, particularly the 'diamond men', were well-educated and infinitely more intelligent than their warders. The minimum mandatory sentence for I.D.B. was five years and ten-year sentences were frequent — a spur to escape, and the prison authorities hit on an effective method to reduce the risk of convicts plotting to make a break for it. Neither the word nor the concept of 'apartheid' had yet been thought of, so when the convicts were herded into their dormitory cells at night each white prisoner was chained between two blacks. There were still escapes, but remarkably few; and of those who did get away, only a handful retained their freedom — most were recap-

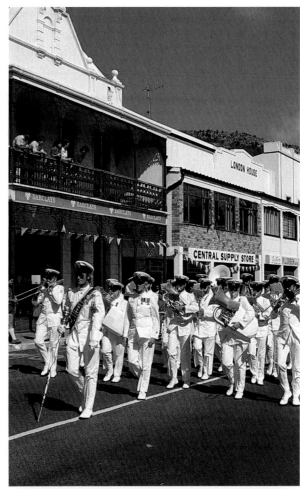

51

52

59

A growing consciousness of the environment came too late to save many creatures which once bred and thrived in the Peninsula. The Cape lion is extinct, and hippo and leopard are no more; even the larger raptors now are rare; but of other birds a multitude remain to gladden the ornithologist – as a weaver builds its nest (53), pelicans sail serenely across a vlei (54) or gulls squabble over a roadside morsel (55). And though the estuarine waters of Sandvlei have been tamed to meet the needs of Marina da Gama (56), ecological studies have guided this development to ensure that man and nature live in harmony and balance.

tured and returned to the breakwater to face the triangle and its dreaded accompaniment, the cat-o-nine-tails, as well as a long stretch in 'solitary'.

Misdemeanours were punished by 'grinding air', as the prisoners termed a spell on the treadmill. The rusting framework and crumbling treads of this futile machine of torture – every bit as mediaeval as the rack or thumbscrew – still stood in the exercise quadrangle of the prison in the late 1940s. For all I know, it may still be there. I have never returned: one visit inside those grim walls was enough to last a lifetime.

The original breakwater has been extended several times, but by 1867 it was 546 metres long and substantial enough for work to start on the first basin. This was named after Victoria's second son, Prince Alfred, who on his second visit to the Cape with the South Atlantic Squadron expressed pleasure that his name should be linked to 'so great an undertaking'. Thus it was the 'Alfred Dock' which he officially opened in July 1870 – fully a year after the work had been completed. That November the first mail steamer, the Union liner *Saxon*, berthed in its calm waters – one of her predecessors, *Athens*, had foundered in the great May gale of 1865 – and it soon became clear that the 3,5 hectares of sheltered water was too small to handle the explosion of maritime visitors. For the discovery of the Kimberley diamond fields not only provided the labour to build the port's protection, but generated substantially increased sea traffic, accelerated by the discovery of gold in the Transvaal.

A second, outer dock – the Victoria Basin – was completed in 1895 and such were the pressures to extend the port facilities as rapidly as possible that the engineers did not rely solely on convict labour, and an additional workforce of 600 Africans was inspanned.

Not only did the burgeoning trade generated by the mineral discoveries of the hinterland put pressure on the harbour facilities, but ship-building techniques and the new materials used combined with steam to make larger vessels feasible. And it became clear at an early stage that the existing berths would be inadequate for what were already being spoken of as the giants of the sea – though by today's standards they were small enough. Further pressures were put on the port during the Anglo-Boer War when, according to contemporary reports, vessels 'bearing men and materiel were moored three deep at the quays, and half a hundred more, both steamers and sailing ships, await in the roadstead their turn to pour ashore the sinews of war'. This, too, was the last time that sail outnumbered steam in Table Bay.

These were the formative years of the mailships, and they also saw the merging of the two main shipping interests which served the Cape – the Union and the Castle Steamship Companies – into the Union Castle Line, which for generations of Britons and South Africans was to become synonymous with travel between the United Kingdom and the Cape. Splendid, seaborne hotels whose accommodation ranged from humble Steerage to the pampering of First Class 'de luxe', they reached their apogee of perfected comfort in the late 1950s and early '60s – a final burst of hedonistic glory. Then came the single-class ships of the up-and-coming Safmarine, determined for a bite of the still lucrative mail contract cherry. But rising costs and the swifter competition of the air made them too late to share more than the remnants of the banquet.

In their long hey-day, interrupted only by two world wars, the puce-hulled liners kept their clockwork schedule, and many mourn their passing. Between the wars, when many Cape schools and other educational institutions were staffed by Britons, it was common, almost customary, for many of these expatriates to travel 'home' for Christmas. Given the relatively long leave they enjoyed at the end of each academic year, they had time to make the 14-day Union Castle voyage to Southampton, to spend the festive season at 'home' and then enjoy the leisurely return trip. Women holiday-makers particularly, could replenish their stock of underwear for the coming year more cheaply in London or Edinburgh than in Cape Town, and so their 'unmentionables' could be worn for the last time and then discarded – unwashed. 'Camiknickers, brassières, petticoats – even the corsets of some of our plumper compan-

56 ▶

ions – all were thrown out of the portholes with gay abandon – at night, of course', one such voyager remembered. 'On each homeward journey enough lingerie must have been discarded to stock a church jumble sale.'

Increasing running costs, declining passenger traffic and the first shadows of containerisation were soon to number the days of the mailships, but the Suez Crisis brought such a bustle of activity to Table Bay and its spreading quays and anchorages that even the most hectic days of the World War II convoys had not seen. Denied the shorter route to Europe which the Suez Canal provided, tankers, passenger liners, regular cargo carriers and tramps bound to and from the East repeated the pattern of their predecessors in the days of sail, calling at the Tavern of the Seas for stores, bunkering and repairs. Maritime engineering works and shipwrights toiled round the clock; ships' chandlers, their bonded wares culled from almost every corner of the globe, waxed liberal with their rounds of drinks as never before. In the bars and nightclubs the cash tills tinkled happily for the free-spending sailormen on brief shore leave, and even the prostitutes had never had it so good. And in the roadstead ships of the world's seafaring nations lay at anchor – sometimes 50 or more – waiting their turn at the quays.

Accordingly a massive expansion programme for the docks was initiated, providing a vast area of protected water which eventually embraced 279,8 hectares, dwarfing to insignificance the original Alfred Basin which it included. Floating cranes, a magnificent modern control tower and Port Captain's office – even a special tanker basin – brought a sleek look to the historic harbour in the 1970s. The Tavern was prepared for anything, but by the time the feast

57

was prepared and the table laid, most of the guests were gone. For the Suez Crisis, which had brought the wild-cat boom to the Tavern had also sown strong seeds of change in the type of ships. Supertankers have become mega-tankers which, while too large for the re-opened Suez Canal, are also more comfortable rounding the Cape at a distance; they have no need to refuel and their victualling is handled by helicopter ferries as they pass, often far below the horizon. The old cargo vessels, so long the backbone of the world's maritime traffic, were ousted by the more efficient and less labour-intensive container ships. And in a contracting world, ever conscious of time, there was no longer a place for the regular liner between the Cape and Europe.

The docks are still busy today, but they seem empty, and much of the glamour has gone, for 'ro-ro' efficiency lacks grace, and there is little magic in the drab trawlers of the Japanese or Taiwan fishing fleets. No more can small boys scuff their toes against the bollards holding thigh-thick hawsers, count the stern-post 'dusters' of a score of nations, or listen to the tattooed sailormen, sea-tanned in grubby singlets, as they call to one another in a multi-lingual babel. No more can their ears prick to the joking call – heard wistfully, half-seriously: 'Hey, Johnny! You want sign as cabin boy?'

But still sometimes, the waters of the harbour and the bay thrill to the snap of sail and the thrum of rigging: when the fleet of yachts sets sail on some trans-ocean race or, better still, when a fine four-masted training ship glides into the haven like a wraith escaped from the nineteenth century, to moor in Table Mountain's shadow. What matter then that the quayside is stacked with duty-free transistor radios and television sets rather than barrels of Constantia, bales of skins or ostrich feathers? The brightwork gleams, the yards are dressed and the elegant curve of clipper ships and windjammers returns down the years to grace the visitors' bows.

The docks are much quieter now and the sounds of night are but the slam of taxi doors and the calls of foreign trawlermen or of the doxies they have found ashore. But the fierce gales still carry the gull-cries of long dead mariners. . . and, in a lull, you may still hear the windlass creak, the concertina wheeze, and the rum-touched shantying of the Tavern's bygone days.

From Muizenberg to Simon's Town the southern suburbs railway, carrying its daily quota of commuters, follows the coast. Spring tides bring the splash of spume to carriage windows, and summer sees each train disgorge a stream of holiday-makers at the beach resorts which mark its track. With the station only a beach-ball throw away from its tidal pool and gaily-coloured changing huts, St James (57) is ever popular. Here in the early mornings a handful of bathers brave the sea, rain or shine, throughout the year – sharing in the 'season' their sunrise exercise with another group of regulars, urchins with home-made sieves who sweep the sands for any coins or other valuables that the previous day's visitors may have lost. But even at the height of the summer crush, a couple can find a pocket of isolation (if only of their own making) on a stretch of beach where surfers throng with brightly-coloured boards (58).

59. *The Fairest Cape assumes an ominous air from this perspective off the Point: a rocky finger beckoning unwary mariners towards disaster, despite its warning lighthouses. The upper beacon is used no longer – the clouds which often mask Da Gama Peak negated its value – but the lower light is the most powerful in the southern hemisphere.*

Cape Point: The phantom of the Cape of Storms

When the moon is full and the sea a beaten pewter broken only by the froth of breaking waves and the wind stirs the fynbos around the foot of the old, deserted Cape Point light, Vasco da Gama peak is an eerie spot. Across the veld some distant clank of a broken branch on corrugated iron is transformed to the metallic rattle of sword hilt on cuirass as Bartholomew Diaz and his men clamber the sandy slope above Maclear beach to plant a *padrao* – long since vanished – and claim the land for Christ and Portugal.

And when the mist descends, tangible, damp and clinging, one feels that the swirling greyness is peopled by other ghosts – the shades of mariners whose ships were devoured by the rocks and angry seas of this south-westernmost stretch of coast. The wind shifts and the distant sound changes, distorted by the fog, its position less precise, the tone now the anguished grate of metal plates on submerged Bellows Rock, the hungriest of all. A startled blacksmith plover adds its anvil clink to the clamour and the blocks of a liner's davits dance emptily.

They are all that is left of the Portuguese liner *Lusitania* which foundered on the Bellows in calm seas on an April midnight in 1911. And it was largely as a result of this disaster that the present lighthouse was built closer to sea-level on a rocky promontory which in rough weather and from a small vessel seems to float just above the waves. For, when *Lusitania* struck, the pall of mist that so frequently forms on the higher ground obscured the lighthouse's warning beam and the ship – with her 200 passengers, and 450 indentured labourers bound for the plantations of São Tomé – had steamed unawares to her doom. An alert lighthouse-keeper spotted her distress maroons and notified the harbour authorities in Simon's Town before making the treacherous descent to the rocks, armed with his own warning lights.

He was too late to prevent the first of the lifeboats from attempting to reach the shore and capsizing in the rock-torn, swirling waters, but in time to haul its half-drowned occupants to safety. Alerted by his signals, the other lifeboats stood out to sea and they were rescued by the Simon's Town tug *Scotsman* and *HMS Forte* of the South Atlantic Station. The keeper's prompt action undoubtedly saved many lives – only one crewman and three passengers perished in the disaster – and his quick thinking and brave rescue efforts earned him a medal and £50 from the Portuguese government. And for many years afterwards each time one of *Lusitania's* sister ships passed Cape Point, three siren blasts saluted both the lighthouse-keeper and the wreck, which was washed from the Bellows by heavy swell four days after foundering.

Cape Point has seen other disasters since then, but the 'new' light, built beneath the treacherous mist, its 19-million candlepower beacon still the most powerful in the southern hemisphere, has made the 'Cape of Storms' safer for shipping and still plays a vital navigational rôle despite the scientific gadgetry which aids the modern mariner.

Ghostly vessels, too, are said to sail the seas around this southern rocky claw of the Peninsula. It is in these waters that the blasphemous Van der Decken is doomed to beat fruitlessly against the winds and current until Judgement Day, his legend nurtured by mariners for almost two and a half centuries before Wagner immortalised the Dutch captain's plight in *Der Fliegende Holländer*.

Van der Decken set sail from Amsterdam for the East Indies in 1600, but because of a damaged rudder became separated from the small fleet of Dutch vessels somewhere west of the Cape. Neither he, his crew, nor his ship was ever again seen – in the flesh.

Legend has it that in a gale soon after the other ships had sailed on, *Flying Dutchman* lost almost all her canvas and was then tossed aimlessly in the Cape rollers for days on end. Food and water ran low as the vessel, now under jury rig, beat vainly to round the Point and make a landfall. In his desperation, Van der Decken cursed the Almighty and vowed that he would round the Cape 'though I should cruise until the Judgement Day'. At this, with the inevitability of all good legends, the Angel of the Lord appeared and – perhaps intent on confounding the future agnostic Wagner as much as punishing Van der Decken – condemned him to 'keep endless vigil while Time itself shall last'.

One suspects that this particular messenger may have been something of a misogynist for there is nothing of the Wagnerian suggestion of salvation through the love of a good woman, nor for that matter of shore leave every seven years in which to find one. The late Professor Erik Chisholm once remarked: 'The Angel was kind, at that. After all, he might have sentenced the poor devil to sitting through an entire performance of the Ring Cycle – without intervals.' But in seamen's myth it is quite clear Van der Decken and his ship must sail 'while Time itself shall last'.

And so they do, if many sober and impeccable sources – including the late King George V – are to be believed. For sightings of *Flying Dutchman,* or a ship answering remarkably closely to her legendary description, have been recorded with surprising frequency. In 1879 the officers, passengers and crew of the steamer *Pretoria* saw an 'old-fashioned ship, her masts and yards bare of all sails', burning blue distress lights, but when the liner altered course to go to the stricken vessel's assistance, it disappeared. The ailing ship materialized again less than two years later in July, when the future King George V (then a midshipman) and several others on *HMS Bachante* – including the look-out – saw the phantom brig. In his diary the then Prince of Wales wrote: 'The look-out man on the forecastle reported her as close to the port bow, where also the officer of the watch saw her surrounded in a strange red light as of a phantom ship all aglow, in the midst of which light the mast, spars and sails of a brig two hundred yards distant stood out in strong relief as she came up.'

Two other Royal Naval vessels accompanying *Bachante* logged their sightings of the same craft in distress and her abrupt vanishing. The Prince appears to have been in no doubt that the brig was *Flying Dutchman*. And with teenage enthusiasm – or a royal disregard for tradition – embellished the legend with his personal touch. Less than 12 hours after he had reported seeing the phantom, *Bachante's* look-out fell from the rigging and broke his neck – thus, according to the Prince, fulfilling 'the curse that he who first sees the ship shall die'. As far as I can establish this is the only reference to the damnation of Van der Decken having any side effects, fatal or otherwise.

Both the *Bachante* and *Pretoria* sightings were after dusk. But one summer's day more than 40 years later, what many believe to have been the spectral ship was seen off Glencairn by numerous holiday makers who included a group of Sunday School children on their annual outing to the seaside. In the heavy summer's warmth, False Bay lay flat calm, without enough wind to shift a thin, ethereal stratum of mist which blurred the outline of the distant Hottentots-Holland mountains. Suddenly the watchers were stirred to interest as what appeared to be a fine full-rigged ship emerged from the mist. She carried little canvas and was quite unlike the few large sailing vessels that still plied the waters off the Cape.

According to a Press report the following day, the ship 'with her sails drawing well, although there was not a breath of wind at the time, appeared to be standing in towards Muizenberg'. 'With uncanny volition' recorded the now defunct *British South Africa Annual* for 1939, 'the ship sailed steadily on until the Glencairn beach folk, now shaken from their lethargy, were standing about, keenly discussing the whys and wherefores of the vessel, which seemed to be bent on self-destruction somewhere on the sand of Strandfontein. Just as excitement reached its climax, however, the mystery ship vanished into thin air as strangely as it had come.'

An explanation was advanced the following day: what the watchers at Glencairn had seen was a mirage and the 'mystery ship' was, by some process of light refraction, the image of a ship which was actually sailing some hundreds of miles away. Scientists may still insist that what people sunning themselves on the beach at Glencairn saw was a manifestation of the laws of refraction. Indeed, ships have been sighted in this way at great distances, notably a P. & O. mailship bound for India and 'seen' at Aden at a time when her log subsequently showed her to have been at least 200 miles away and when no similar ship was nearby. However, many that day on the False Bay shore were satisfied that what they had seen was Van der Decken's spectral vessel.

A few years ago I tried to track down some of those spellbound sunbathers. I felt that they could not have been subjects of a mass hallucination – sun-drugged perhaps but nothing more, and not with a Sunday School group among their number. I was unsuccessful, but in the course of research turned up another, later sighting. In 1942 an invalid living at Camps Bay saw from her balcony a strange sailing ship 'in difficulties and only a few hundred yards off shore'. There appeared to be only a solitary figure on the deck and, by the time she had hobbled indoors and returned with binoculars, the ship had disappeared. She reported what she had seen to the police and they, in turn, informed the coastal defence authorities.

Her telephone call generated frenzied activity at Naval Headquarters which was seriously concerned by a series of mysterious losses of merchantmen – later established to have been the victims of U-boats. Patrol boats were ordered out to search the approaches to Table Bay, but could find nothing untoward – let alone a somewhat battered sailing ship.

Not for them the stuff of centuries-old legends. But the lady concerned was convinced that what she had seen was *Flying Dutchman*. And I for one choose to believe her and echo the William Plomer lines:

And still in the storm, as sailors say,
Sere and wan and white as bone,
The phantom ship drives against the gale,
And an old man stands on the poop alone.

The fynbos scrub of the Cape Point Nature Reserve supports a wealth of creatures including the ostrich (**60**), introduced and breeding here though never laying such large clutches of eggs as its Karoo counterparts, and the bontebok (**61**), once threatened by extinction but now protected in reserves such as this and the Bontebok National Park, near Swellendam. But it is the Cape Point baboons which capture the attention of most visitors; small family groups gambol or sun themselves on the rocks of the roadside verge, while others patrol the edges of the parking area in search of scraps or titbits – for despite large notices prohibiting the feeding of baboons, there are invariably visitors who do (**62**).

62

Robben Island: A place of loneliness in many guises

Heavy winds, dark with rain and bearing the chill of their passage across South Atlantic's icy waters, batter the stunted trees. Beneath them, disorderly as a child's dominoes thrust randomly into the sand, are the old gravestones – slate, with incised lettering almost erased by the action of the salt-laden wind; wood, polished to the anonymity of a driftwood plank. But these haphazard, meagre memorials record the end of lives marked by anguish and pain; for the cemetery is that of Robben Island: fortress, prison, leper station, limbo of political exiles, and the site of the first, short-lived, attempts at permanent white settlement at the Cape.

There had been temporary 'settlements' in the *Tafel Vallei* for almost a century before Van Riebeeck arrived to establish his victualling station for the VOC. Portuguese seafarers had given the Cape a wide berth since the death of Admiral de Almeida in 1510 in a fracas with a Hottentot clan on the shores of Table Bay, but sealers and whalermen of many nations had made it a temporary base for their bloody task of harvesting blubber and pelts. However, what was intended as a 'permanent' settlement – and would have been the first on the southern tip of Africa – was not established until 1611, when King James I of England shipped a group of convicts to this small, low-lying outcrop of Malmesbury Shale. Two reprieved murderers – both youths and apparently the mildest and gentlest of the party – were among the petty thieves and debtors marooned to found this new British colony, as to whose numbers contemporary accounts do not agree. However, 14 men – 'all in pitiful condition' – were eventually returned to England, their reluctant attempt defeated by bleak conditions and ravages of climate.

The castaways did not starve, though their diet must have been somewhat repetitive. Seals and sea birds' eggs were abundant, and there were fair numbers of sheep, for it was customary for ships which had called into the bay to leave lean livestock to graze the coarse island grasses and take off with them a similar number of fattened animals. No predators threatened them, and the rip-tide currents which surrounded the waters daunted the Hottentots – reluc-

tant navigators at the best of times – from attempting the crossing. Oppressed by their isolation, two groups – one led by Dartmouth shop-keeper Jon Kynge – built cockleshell rafts on which they attempted the narrower but more dangerous crossing from the island's only landing place at Murray's Bay to the mainland near Blaauwberg. Kynge's small raft capsized before reaching the half-way mark. The crew were 'devoured before our helpless eyes by ferocious fish [sharks] larger than we recollected ever seeing', one of the castaways was to record many years later. The other group foundered on the ragged-toothed reefs that fringe the Blaauwberg beach 'but on swimming to the shore were set upon and clubbed by the natives, suffering as swift and bloody a demise as had their predecessors at the hands of the cannibal fish'.

Today the currents, sharks and rock-girt shores which combine to make the island so inaccessible have encouraged its return to one of its earliest rôles – the detention of 'political' prisoners. Do the ghosts of Batavian princes, political and religious exiles from the Spice Isles of the East, or even of scarred and grizzled mutineers, peer through the chain-link fences at the blocks of cells bathed in their guardian spot-lights?

Certainly the island was an eerie place in the immediate post-War years, when its only inhabitants were the lighthouse keeper and his family of 11 children ('There's not much else to do', he once explained to me with earthy candour) and a handful of maintenance artillerymen caring for the coastal gun and searchlight relics of the War. Nodding arums carpeting marshier patches of scrub could not completely dispel the gloom, and even the lolloping rabbits – introduced by Van Riebeeck as a source of fresh meat, and proliferated by a three-century population explosion – made one think of convicts' snares rather than of Beatrix Potter.

At night, despite a full moon and two old-fashioned bicycle lamps, the cemetery was a fearsome place. A sock caught on the remnant of a grave's edging seemed as if clutched in the ghoulish grip of a long-dead leper's stump; the distant clank of the island's only windmill I knew with a 12-year-old's certainty to be the rattle of a convict's irons. Fleeing the dark, I tripped in one of the rabbit burrows that dot the sparse topsoil of this place of ghosts. A twisted ankle lent some dignity to my return to Cape Town four days early, chugging across the choppy waters of Table Bay in *Issie,* the splendid old wooden vessel that served as both supply and passenger craft to the island's tiny population. It was my first visit to Robben Island, and the premature departure cost me the chance of finding any of the 'Post Office' stones which were placed on the island decades before their use on the shores of Table Bay. It remains a bleak memory.

Yet the 5,2-square-kilometre outcrop saw happy times as well. Van Riebeeck settled a superintendent with a party of men there, not as a punishment but to tend the animals, collect shells for the mainland lime kilns, and quarry and dress the local stone used in building the fledgling mainland town and described as 'excellent slate-coloured stone, that is little inferior to marble and beautifully veined'. The Company employees set to this task were also charged to keep a careful watch for the arrival of any VOC ships and, should an evening landfall seem likely, light a signal bonfire for their benefit. By 1657 the commander had ordered a permanent signal beacon built and this was lit each night, so establishing the first permanent navigational aid on the South African coast.

63

*Only a few kilometres of water (**64**) separate Robben Island from the jut of the mainland shore at Sea Point. Yet strong currents, the threat of sharks and the cruel outcrops of shale fringing much of the island deter all but the strongest swimmer and strengthen its present use as a prison, where warders (**63**) stroll – and patrol – the waterline.*

64

A MELTING POT OF PEOPLE

66

Her contemporaries – cities which also had their origins in the colonial and mercantile needs of the nations of Europe – seem to take pride in their lack of pretensions, but Cape Town retains a façade of self-conscious dignity. New York may rejoice in its polyglot, raz-mattaz European origins, Sydney in its brash and dubious antecedents, Buenos Aires in its avaricious and wicked past, but South Africa's mother city turns to the world a face of quiet, almost demure, charm. Yet of all the earth's cities she may well be called the most truly cosmopolitan, the men and women who moulded her more varied in nation, faith and colour perhaps than those of any other settlement. It was the Dutch first, and later the British, who exerted the strongest influence in her shaping but she, the most southerly of Africa's cities, was touched at one time or other by the Khoi-San, West and East Africans, Portuguese, Indonesians, Spanish, French, German, Indian, Italian, Scandinavian – sometimes briefly, at others for good; sometimes by only a handful of people, at others in an immigrant flood; but all left some indelible mark on the city.

Today both she and her people enjoy a reputation for insularity – almost of reserve – which is not entirely undeserved, for the Mother City seems to look down on her younger South African relatives with some disdain – by-blows which if ignored may keep their distance, tolerated but not entitled to share the inheritance of the western Cape. The dignified dowager seems to frown disapprovingly at the materialism of her northern offspring, Johannesburg, no less than at the hedonistic indulgence of her eastern cousin, Durban, forgetting – as the old do – her own hoyden past. For she has not always been a dowager, not always sedate – and even today, she sometimes forgets her dignity. Milkmaid, harlot, cinderella, fishwife, tavern doxy, grande dame. . . Cape Town has been all of them – and at times still is.

And a city is its people, shaped by their heritage and flavoured by their tastes: and the more diverse their cultures, the richer its colours, and – perhaps contrarily – the deeper their various preconceptions, the fewer their shared prejudices. For although the Capetonians have a reputation for reserve, they were in many ways and for many years a people – regardless of the colour of their skin – remarkably free from prejudice. A process of multiple symbiosis created a unique population with its own mélange of culture and tradition that the Capetonian born not only inherits but breathes daily with his dose of seaside ozone or city-centre exhaust fumes. Perhaps this is why he feels apart from his fellow South Africans, and has gained his reputation for insularity.

'The bundu begins just beyond Bellville,' grumbled an elderly Mother City journalist when told that he was being transferred on promotion to Durban. Any Capetonian, whatever his colour, would understand this *cri de coeur*.

The Peninsula's first human inhabitants are remembered only in their stone artifacts, their refuse middens and a few converted fish-traps, but the Bushmen and Hottentots who followed them and were encountered by the first white visitors came from far beyond that very 'bundu'. Both were Khoi-San peoples: the Bushman, hunter-gatherers; and the Hottentots, mainly-nomadic pastoralists of whom one small clan which combed the beaches in Van Riebeeck's day and known as 'strandlopers', led an existence closer to that of the Bushman.

Squeezed by the inexorable advance of land-hungry whites who, in the earlier stages at least, regarded these small milk-chocolate and honey-coloured people as 'sub-human', and the territorial drive of the Bantu-speaking tribes from the north-east who enslaved, absorbed or killed them, the Bushman numbers diminished. Those left found sanctuary in the wasteland deserts of the northwest to which their Stone-Age existence was suited, and where groups continue to eke an existence today.

The Hottentots also faced similar pressures, and their closer, more persistent contact with the whites added the ravages of disease and internecine wars. Their more advanced, pastoral way of life denied them the desert option and they exist no longer – though a few of their descendants are still to be found in rural areas, and sometimes a 'typical hottentot' face is still to be seen among the Coloured community of the Peninsula.

65 *(previous page). Whether waiting patiently to watch a passing parade, or less patiently to cross a traffic-busy thoroughfare, the features of any group of the Mother City's children mirror their diverse origins.*

67

*Against a richly ornate background that bears tangible witness to their religious and cultural heritage, a Muslim and his grandson (**66**) kneel in worship in one of the many mosques which dot the city. The white skull caps, or onderkappies, of the faithful were originally worn under the fez – tasselled in the case of a* haji *or one who had made the pilgrimage to Mecca. Save on special occasions, such as weddings or funerals, few Muslims wear the fez today; instead the skull caps have become increasingly ornate and are often elaborately embroidered or crocheted in intricate patterns. Thus on Fridays, when from minarets like this (**67**) the faithful are called to prayer, Rose Street and the surrounding lanes and alleys become streams of bobbing white, as young Cape Malays jostle and joke on their way to one of the city's mosques.*

68

7

69

7

74

68-75. *Whether it is the exuberant high spirits of an 'intervarsity' rugby match or the more solemn happiness of a Malay wedding feast, the nonchalant contemplation of the world through the drifting smoke of a hawker's cigarette or the oblivious concentration of two chess opponents, the faces of Capetonians reflect as wide a range of mood as that of their ancestry.*

74

75

These yellow-skinned people made a lasting physical impression on Cape Town's population, but of all its progenitors they left the least cultural mark: a few words for objects or places rather than concepts. Yet had it not been for the Hottentot tribes it is unlikely that Van Riebeeck's tiny settlement would have survived. It was they who had fat-tailed sheep and 'horned cattle' which the settlement could obtain by barter — even if the original owners had the exasperating habit of stealing back the livestock soon after a deal had been concluded: and their knowledge of edible indigenous plants helped the garrison over a bleak period of scurvy when their first plantings failed. The head of one clan in particular, Herry, was an almost daily visitor, although his penchant for other people's property led to varying periods of banishment.

In spite of the Hottentots' cavalier attitude towards the legal ownership of sheep and cattle — which led to several sporadic skirmishes in the early years of the settlement — there was an essentially comfortable relationship between the Dutch and the indigenous people. Clan headmen were often honoured guests at the garrison, sharing the board with the Commander and his senior officials, though their table manners left much to be desired, for they were 'less delicate even in their treatment of food than is the least educated of peasants'.

Fun-loving and untroubled by the Protestant work ethic, the Hottentots soon earned a reputation for laziness which was compounded by their craving for strong drink and tobacco. Even the children of the families living near the wood-and-sod fort developed a liking for these dubious benefits of civilization, and when the first school opened for the children of slaves and Hottentots a tot of brandy and an inch of tobacco were the daily inducement for the pupils to attend. Several Hottentots became gargantuan alcoholics and early records indicate that even minor chiefs were often briefly imprisoned for drunkenness.

Best remembered of these early topers is Hottentot Eva, though she took to the bottle only late in life and then probably as an escape from intolerable pressures. She was named by the settlers, who found the tongue-twisting clicks of !Kro!toa impossible to pronounce, and was Herry's niece and the protégée of Maria de la Quellerie, the Commander's wife. Only about ten years old when she was 'adopted' — not quite a servant nor accepted as a member of the family — Eva already had a smattering of Portuguese and soon picked up enough Dutch to be invaluable as an interpreter in Van Riebeeck's dealings with the local clans. And though the first settlers lacked the missionary zeal of some of the later arrivals at het Balk [hamlet] de Tafel valleij, Maria seems to have included an element of religious instruction in Eva's training, at least enough for her to have been baptised soon before the Van Riebeecks were promoted to Batavia.

She was not the first Hottentot convert — the educational carrot of brandy and tobacco was remarkably successful in diverting heathen souls — but she was probably the first to begin to understand the meaning of Christianity and its moral concepts. This may or may not have ensured her Heavenly future, but it certainly opened the matrimonial portals, and two years later in 1664 she became the wife of Pieter van Meerhoff, a Danish mercenary who had risen through the ranks of the VOC's private army to become assistant surgeon. The new Mevrou van Meerhoff was in fact a figure of some social importance and the nuptials at the fort were celebrated with 'considerable festivity'.

Seen through the eye of today's racial prejudice this first 'official' marriage across the colour line may seem strange. But then there was little or no disdain of the Hottentots because of skin colour, although their customs and even personal habits differed radically from those of even the Europeans lowliest in the social order. There had of course been liaisons — despite Van Riebeeck's stern ordinance that the only contact between Hottentots and the garrison should be through him and his senior officials — and visitors during the early days of settlement remarked on the red and blonde hair of some of the 'mulatto' children. Given the small proportion of women among the first 125 whites to make their home at the Cape, such liaisons — and later, intermarriages — were understandably inevitable.

Transformed from an oil company's headquarters – an impressively modern block at the time of its building, but long since overtaken by the streamlining of contemporary architecture – a comfortable hotel looks out across the cobbled expanse of Greenmarket Square where once the farmers came to sell their produce. A ground-floor terrace restaurant (76) is a popular meeting place for the city's younger set, giving coolth in summer and protection from the winter's rains. But whatever the weather there is little protection, save a muffler or issued rain-suit, for the city's paper sellers (77) who make raucous the city centre's intersections with their cries: 'Kaytoy, Eeburgee, Argee. . .'

This lack of potential brides worried the authorities, for though the *Here XVII* had no intention of colonizing the Cape, their commercial need of a settlement in *Tafel Vallei* made a reasonably content and stable community essential: which they were convinced would be best achieved through matrimony. If there were not enough women at the Cape, some would have to be imported from Europe.

'Apart from the shortage of labour, there was a real demand for women', Martin Lichtenstein was later to record with for him unusual accuracy. 'Also here the mother country helped. From the orphanages of Amsterdam, Rotterdam and Delft 50 honest girls were selected who voluntarily travelled in 1657 to the Cape, to find husbands there and become mothers of a new people.'

During the settlement's first decade, surrogate 'wives' at least were easier to obtain than labour, for the Hottentots' concept of life and the work ethic of the Europeans were totally different. Nor did the *Kaapmans* wish to change their ways; the women foraged for *veldkos* and tilled what little land was cultivated; their sons tended the herds and flocks; and the men, when not indulging in minor skirmishes with their neighbours, were quite content with their 'place in the sun', preferably with a pipe of 'wild tobacco' in one hand and – since the advent of the Dutch – better still with something alcoholic in the other.

Van Riebeeck coaxed and cajoled, bribed and browbeat, but the few indigenous people he managed to enlist in his labour force were desultory workers, had little idea of time-keeping, and – judging by the high incidence of absenteeism – were related to an endless supply of frail and sickly aged whose funerals occurred with unpredictable but monotonous frequency. The Hottentots were, in fact, not only lazy but work-shy. Nor were the 90 VOC soldiers – nor for that matter any of the artisans who accompanied Van Riebeeck – particularly enthusiastic about clearing ground, heaving wood, or quarrying and transporting rock.

Faced with an historic problem, Van Riebeeck and his successors sought an equally historic solution – the use of slaves – and in doing so laid the groundwork for an ethnic and a cultural transfusion which was to have an impact on the Peninsula and the Boland out of all proportion to the numbers introduced in this way here. It was to put its own unique stamp on the city, for the Cape Malays were to give their exotic touch to almost *every* facet of life – first in the settlement and later throughout the city. The Dutch had never been a slaving nation in the sense of their merchantmen carrying cargoes of 'black ivory' for profit, but the concept was well-established and their Far Eastern settlements owed much of their efficiency to the slaves of the Company and of its officials.

As early as 1655 three house-slaves had been brought to Table Bay from Madagascar, which, with Delagoa Bay, was to remain the central source of fresh slaves until emancipation in 1838. But the first ones used in the Cape for hard physical labour arrived in March 1658 on *Amersfoort,* a VOC ship which had 'taken them off a Portuguese vessel' – 170 of them, all West Africans, who soon proved almost more trouble than they were worth. Not only were they as reluctant to work as the Hottentots, but many had the habit of running away, thus further reducing the limited work force, and involving parties of soldiers being detailed to recapture them.

This lack of labour was a problem which was never really solved, and which in its way continues today, when the city and its environs must still rely on migrant or contract workers to help turn its industrial wheels. The *Here XVII* had readily agreed to Van Riebeeck's proposal to use slaves – and were later to encourage Commandants and Governors to impress 'spare' able-bodied men from the passing fleets – but their general attitude towards the settlement in *Tafel Vallei* compounded the problem. The Company was not interested in colonization; they were merchants, and the settlement had only been established on the shores of Table Bay to serve as a sea-route staging-post and haven for the VOC fleets, and to provide fresh supplies for their crews. Even in the East, Dutch territorial aspirations were dictated by the requirements of trading profits, whereas at the Cape there were no riches to acquire, so there was

Nourished by a climate that favours outdoor activities, South Africans in general are reputedly obsessed by sport; they have elevated rugby and cricket, in particular, to almost religious proportions. Capetonians are no exception. Give them a test match or Currie Cup final at Newlands and the city's offices miraculously half empty – as though a multitude of grandparents had died in sudden holocaust. And if rugby and cricket are our minor gods, their acolytes are sunbronzed macho hearties such as these (78). Found singly or in droves on any beach, they jog, sprint and flaunt their tans – perhaps preparing for tomorrow's game. . . or possibly to catch some 'dolly's' eye?

no need to expand – save where it served the VOC's commercial objectives. In fact Amsterdam agreed only with reluctance to the establishment of Free Burghers – in effect the first real citizens of the Peninsula – because of the benefits which were to accrue to their pockets.

The Company had nothing to lose and everything to gain. Conditions towards the end of February 1657 under which the first nine men were granted manumission from what had been little better than a form of 'paid slavery' favoured their former masters. The 11,5 hectares of land allotted to each one tax-free for 12 years was untamed bush on the banks of the Liesbeeck River – and was mortgaged to the Company against the initial supplies it provided; the Free Burghers were charged the current market prices obtaining in the Netherlands for the equipment and seed which they bought on credit from the Company; the Company dictated the prices these founder farmers were paid for their produce – it was the only outlet they had; the Company kept a tight rein on trade with the Hottentots; and, above all, from the Company's point of view, it substantially reduced its overheads, saving both the men's wages and the rations issued not only to them but their wives and children – for one of the Company's stipulations governing the freeing of the burghers from its service was that each should be married. The four families which settled at Groeneveld, in the vicinity of present-day Newlands, under the leadership of Herman Remajenne, and the five under Steven Jansen (or Botma, as he was later known) at De Hollandsche Thuyn, near what is today Mowbray, had in effect exchanged one form of servitude for another, harder, submission to the same masters. In everything but name they were little more than agricultural labourers. They were encouraged to buy slaves, again on credit, but generally found them to be as ineffectual in the 'free' fields as they had proved in their labours for officialdom. Moreover, the slaves they bought were usually the laziest or most intractable, who more often than not had to be returned to the Company within a few months, either traded in for (hopefully) more efficient ones, or written off as a loss by the farmer concerned who still owed the VOC for the services rendered during the time he owned them.

The farmers' lot was not easy; in many ways they were worse off than the poorest peasants in the Netherlands. Their accommodation was primitive and they were often harried by the Hottentots, for their farmsteads had become – as the Company had foreseen – the buffer 'frontier' between the garrison and its gardens and the tribesmen. Yet as the first Europeans to own individual and freehold land in the Peninsula – and thus in southern Africa – they were as much the founders of a nation as the Pilgrim Fathers in the United States. Certainly they deserve the claim of being the first citizens of a city whose existence lay more than 200 years in the future.

What Botma, Remajenne and their fellows lacked in tangible possessions and security they made up with determination, but their venture would have foundered – and the Mother City's history might have taken a different course – had not the Company released others of their servants (this time including bachelors and widowers) to work for themselves. Only a few of these new free burghers opted to work as farm assistants, but there were enough to avert the labour crisis which threatened the future of Groeneveld and De Hollandsche Thuyn, where the wives and children already toiled alongside their menfolk.

The bulk of the new freedmen became artisans, plying their trades as carpenters, tailors and smiths, with the Company's promise of bringing their families to join them in exchange for an undertaking by the men that they would remain at the Cape for 20 years. They formed an urban nucleus around which a village became a town and blossomed to eventual cityhood.

As their cottages and lean-to workshops took shape in the shadow of the fort, a semblance of contemporary European village life came to the settlement for the first time, and with it a sense of permanence. The clash of hammer on iron as Roeloff Zieuwertsen shaped a ploughshare or readied the iron rim for a wagonwheel rang summonses to the Hottentot riff-raff who spent much of the daylight loitering near his smithy – and avoiding the guards – to

79

London has its Petticoat Lane, Paris its Left Bank 'flea market', and while this small section of historic Church Street is a pale shadow of the street stalls of the European capitals, it has its own special charm (79). Modern bric-a-brac, chipped art nouveau statuettes, old coins and antique brass share trestle-table space in improbable harmony among the gallimaufry of goods the vendors display. And for the dedicated browser there is always the possible excitement of a 'find', some valuable trifle which has gone unnoticed by the hawk-eyed experts who carefully check each 'new' offering. If its wares are usually old, the Church Street market is itself relatively new to the Cape Town scene; not so the flower sellers (80) who throughout the year offer an array of blooms that change – but for the dyed dried grasses and everlastings – with the seasons. Their venue and the special water-troughs in which they keep their daily stock, has been moved many times to suit the building needs of the changing city centre, but the sellers form a familiar link with the past; many of those who today offer roses, or 'glads', or 'nations' or 'zinnies', are descendants of folk who sold blooms to the Victorian passersby.

80 ▶

gawp at the fascinating activities of the whites. 'While the heathen were loathe to work, preferring godless idleness and drink, there was never lack of spectators for the good and honest effort of their betters' according to one chronicler.

Except for the presence of the honey-skinned idlers during the day and the night-time chorus of hyaenas punctuated by the occasional contrapuntal bass of lion, life largely resembled that of the villages of the Low Countries, but with the Commandant and his senior officials even more powerful, though on a smaller scale, than their counterparts in the United Netherlands. The social order was clearly defined though it showed little if any of the snobbery that was to mark Peninsula society in later years: when, in a euphoria of wealth, the Bairnsfathers were reputed 'to speak only to God and the Cloete's and the Cloete's speak only to God' – and presumably to the Bairnsfathers. Social rank notwithstanding, there was little room for snobbery among either the garrison or the new villagers; all their efforts were turned to wresting a living – or producing a satisfactory balance sheet for the Company – from trade or from the sometimes hostile environment of *Tafel Vallei*.

Hendrick Boom and his assistants struggled to establish vegetables and later fruit trees in the alien soil; Van Riebeeck and his *Sekunde* struggled to impose the European concept of ownership in their stock dealings with the Hottentots; and the burghers of Groeneveld and De Hollandsche Thuyn toiled to tame the lands they had been granted, harvest enough cereal to meet their obligations and grow enough vegetables to meet the needs of their immediate families. The structure of local society and the design of their low and relatively mean dwellings resembled those many had left behind when taking service with the Company. But here all similarity ended: there was none of the softness, the lush green of northern Europe, the gentle rains that fell predictably and when they were needed, the rich soil that turned easily to the plough. Instead, there were times of drought and times of flood; days when the Southeaster winds tore at the thatch of the *riet*-bound roofs and at the topsoil of the farmlands;

81

82

days when the sun burned mercilessly down on seedlings and saplings to complete the havoc which the wind had begun. Yet there were also times when the land and the climate could be so benign that Van Riebeeck could write in the official journal of the settlement: 'The return ships will find so much here that, not only during their stay will they have abundance, but they will be able to take a large quantity away for the voyage' and, later, exultantly: 'Today, praise be to God, wine was made for the first time from Cape grapes, namely from the new must fresh from the vat' – the record of a successful venture of the Company's which the burghers were quick to emulate.

And with the passage of the years more servants of the Company were 'freed' to take up agriculture, moving further afield to plant their vines and sow corn. Their visits to the settlement to dispose of produce – still to the VOC and at prices fixed by the *Here XVII* – resembled the village market days of the Netherlands, but modified by the hand of Africa which already began to make its indelible mark on the men, women, and children, and their way of life.

Teams of oxen, the son of the family mounted on the *voorloper*, strained against their harness to haul the heavy wagons, built by Zieuwertsen (forgotten today, but perhaps the father of South African industry?) from planks cut by the carpenter-timbermen Lendert Cornelissen or Dirck Vreem in the forests on the slopes above Wynberg or Hout Bay. For some the trek to the fort was only a few hours' journey, but as the farmsteads stretched further into what was to become the Boland, every visit to the settlement was a potentially dangerous adventure. On the open space outside the fort – later the landward side of the Castle – the wagons would outspan and their occupants mingle in a typical market-day crowd, exchanging news and gossip, buying seed from Company officials; perhaps visiting the home of Hendrik van Zurwerden who had set up as tailor, or Wouter Cornelisz Mostert's mill, or the sick attending Jan Vetteman, the garrison surgeon who had been allowed to set up in private practice.

Even the visit of a ship, usually a magnet for all the farmers within a day's journey of the settlement, could not muster gatherings greater than those of a village market. Both the garrison and the burgher population together were pitifully few in comparison with all but the meanest of today's dorps. And when Van Riebeeck left for Batavia, more than five years after the first free burghers were allotted land, the farmers, artisans and their assistants numbered only 35 men, 15 women and 22 children. Even in 1687, 25 years after that, these figures had grown only to 87, 55 and 117 respectively. The settlement's growth strained even further the already-stretched labour resources.

The *Here XVII* reacted to the situation by relaxing their attitude to the settlement, and even encouraged non-Company Netherlands citizens to emigrate to the Cape – again less from a wish to colonize or from a sense of altruism than from their customary pragmatism: a settled burgher population would provide them with a pool of militia, making possible a reduction in the paid garrison.

Attempts begun in 1685 to persuade Netherlands citizens – preferably those with a knowledge of wine and spirit making – to spend 15 years at the Cape fell flat. The home economy was thriving as comfortably as the Company's trade with the East – so much so that the *Here XVII* were turning even more than before to Hessians and Scandinavians to fill the vacant posts in their service. Next they tried to recruit French Protestants who had fled to Holland after the revocation of the Edict of Nantes. Most of these tens of thousands of religious refugees had passed through Holland and settled in Britain, but several thousand had made their homes in the Netherlands where many prospered. But even those struggling to make ends meet were reluctant to venture to a little-known sub-continent peopled with heathen savages and – if the tales which were gradually finding their way into print could be believed – alive with wild creatures better suited to the nightmares of the Apocrypha than Christian dreams of success. Only in 1687, when the period of voluntary exile was reduced to five years, could the Company find any takers – and then, considering the number of French refugees settled in Holland, only a paltry few, who

Conjured by changing winds and a varied topography, quirks of the weather are a feature of the Peninsula's winter climate, and it is not uncommon for prolonged and steady rains to drench the mountain slopes of Newlands while beaches, only a few kilometres distant, bask in balmy sunshine. But there are long days, too, when in a cold front's grip all of Cape Town shivers under a sodden sky, and umbrellas are de rigeur (81) – providing of course they are not blown inside out – and Capetonians long for the springtime easing of their snuffles. But spring and summer have their own quirks: pockets of calm while the South-easter rages, tearing at roofs and uprooting trees in random whimsy. The early white inhabitants dubbed this wind 'the Cape Doctor', believing that it blew away bad vapours that bore disease. Certainly it scoured the streets of the settlement – as it does the Foreshore today – of litter and rubbish where disease may have bred. However, to the pedestrian battling across the concrete canyons which channel the South-easter's blast (82) the 'Doctor's' ministrations seem more baleful than benevolent.

82

83

came in comparatively small groups spread over more than a decade, rather than the mass wave of sophisticated culture that the more romantically inclined historians would have us believe. Records have been lost, and estimates of the numbers of these French refugees in all range from 157 to 200 at the most. But if they had arrived *en masse* the wave would have been large enough to swamp the Dutch community – already mingled with a small German element – and the French peasant cultural shock might have altered the course of development in the Boland and thus, ultimately, in South Africa.

But the transfusions of new blood which began in April 1688 and continued until 1699 were gradual and the cultural impact occurred in a kind of slow two-way osmosis from which both the newcomers and the established settlers benefited. Most of the first arrivals came ashore in Table Bay with few material possessions and virtually nothing in the way of cash, and 'a considerable sum in money and in stock' was raised by local officials and the burghers to help establish them on farms which the authorities – wisely as it transpired – had allotted scattered among the lands of established burghers in the Stellenbosch and Olifantshoek valleys. They made up for what they lacked in material wealth by their willingness to work; their peasant origins had accustomed them to hard physical effort which was precisely what the settlement needed – able, capable and willing labour. And the transfusion came at a time when, but for the newcomers, its agricultural existence might have faltered. Nor can their later chauvinism and almost ceaseless grumbling detract from their important rôle in South Africa's history – especially that of the Peninsula and Boland.

One contribution made by the Huguenots – as these French refugees came to be known – has been exaggerated to a degree. Yet the myth has been perpetuated by generations of school-teachers – presumably named Du Preez, Le Roux, Marais, De Villiers or something of similarly French origin – and a solitary voice is unlikely to explode it. The myth, like so many of the better far-fetched yarns, has vinous origins: though in this case, literally. And it runs thus:

The generally accepted story is that before the arrival of the Huguenots with their viticultural expertise the Dutch agricultural community had produced only poor quality wines and crude, fiery spirits. But the arrival of the French and the knowledge they brought with them had, as it were, an alchemical effect, transmuting 'plonk' into a connoisseur's delight; and, thanks to them, until the years of phylloxera, the wines of the Cape never looked back. . .

The facts are different. Pierre, Jacob and Abraham de Villiers, three brothers originally from La Rochelle and the first of the Huguenots to have any practical experience in European vineyards, did not arrive until May 1689 and their knowledge was essentially that of grafting and cultivation. They knew less about wine-making than the burghers whose community they joined. According to Simon van der Stel who, initially at least, was an ardent protagonist of the French, the effect on wines of these émigré arrivals was in terms of quantity rather than quality. There was more of it – partly because men like the De Villiers used techniques which led to better yields, but mainly because more land was given over to vines. The quality was no better, plonk was still plonk: and though a *vin du pays* is nothing to be ashamed of, it lacks distinction.

It is generally believed, too, that it was the Huguenots who brought with them the 'civilizing' influences of art and good manners to the primitive society of the Cape, creating with their love of literature and music, their furniture and elegant dress, something closer to the graciousness of Europe's upper classes. Again, the reality is very different. Most of the newcomers were of peasant stock with no more social graces than their Dutch counterparts – even the Reverend Pierre Simond who came to the Cape to minister in French to the spiritual needs of the Huguenots had deplorable table manners and 'broke wind vigorously even at the most inopportune times'. And they were too poor to allow for fine furniture or fancy trappings of dress, which were to come later with the prosperity which *all* the burghers shared. So poor indeed were the newcomers that Van der Stel wrote to Batavia requesting that a collection be made for 'these poor people,' and evoking a response both immediate and

Cape Town shares with every other major city the extremes of wealth and poverty, though in her case the line has long been blurred by race and colour, for the Peninsula's inhabitants number some extremely rich blacks as well as poor whites. More tolerant legislation, which would open certain 'white' residential areas to people of colour, may further soften the distinction. But despite the growing purchasing power of the non-white market, the extravagant luxuries are still very much the province of the city's wealthier whites. It is largely they who patronise the haute couture *parades of fashion (83), briefly envying, perhaps, the models' slender youth. . .*

83

generous: the church relief board sent 18 000 guilders which had belonged to the poor-box of the VOC's former island possession Formosa, lost in 1682.

Nor did the Huguenots set much of an example when it came to manners – or if they did it was soon eroded, for there was little sign of it a century later when Lady Anne Barnard (commenting on an impromptu ball near what by then was known as French Hoek) wrote: 'The young dutchmen [sic] of the neighbourhood attended, awkward enough youths indeed, and a dozen of young ladys amongst whom was a lately married Jacobin beauty of the name of Rousseau, of 6 feet high and two inches, broad in proportion – her age is only sixteen so we may prophecy much for her future greatness! – the young women are often good looking at that age, but they all want softness. – When they are, what is supposed here *well* educated, they have great ideas of *keeping up* their dignity and not being *put upon*, which dignity being rather coarsely supported, becomes a Haughty pride. . .' Of the same dance at the Landrosts [sic] Lady Anne goes on to describe the scene at the supper table at which two of the guests quite openly and without any regard for appearances, suckled their 'Moye Kinders' much to their husbands' 'great discomposure'.

Lady Anne, who was not above moments of earthiness herself, obviously sympathised with the nursing mothers, but behaviour of this sort would hardly have been considered acceptable among the middle-class citizens of Paris – or Amsterdam – in the late seventeenth century, let alone the eighteenth (when Lady Anne was writing), and the social mores and manners of the inhabitants of the Peninsula and its adjacent farming areas *were* improving.

But if the Huguenots made little contribution to the wine industry and even less to the grace of Cape life (an omission which a handful of their countrymen were later to rectify with stunningly gratifying results), they left a permanent

*. . .before returning in the family's 'second' car to their homes in one of the 'better' suburbs (**84**). Here spacious gardens act as buffer zones, protecting each inhabitant from the nuisance of neighbours' dogs, the squawls of neighbours' children; domestic help is still plentiful, though sufficiently problematical to head the list of tea-time topics; and bridge is played as much for face as pleasure in the halcyon world of those who've earned – perhaps undeservingly – the epithet: 'the idle rich'.*

imprint on the character of that life quite out of proportion to their relatively small numbers. The example of their industriousness, and their contribution as catalysts in achieving political change proved vitally more important. Their new homes and the future they foresaw lay among the farming community, and it was here that their presence became felt, while their direct influence in the development of the Peninsula and its embryo town was slight.

Politico-religious refugees from Europe provided extra muscle and the energy needed to develop the land, and it was such exiles from the East who helped to shape the city. This time it was the Dutch who were the oppressors rather than the haven: benign, paternalistic almost, yet oppressors none the less. The *Here XVII's* seal of approval for slavery did little to help the agricultural labour force, but the successive influence of slaves from the East – Java, Macassar, and the Malay Peninsula – gave a new dimension to the population of the settlement in *Tafel Vallei* and expanded immensely the skills available to it. For these slaves, generally referred to as 'Malays', were very different from the Malagasy and African labour. For nearly a century they came: as house servants and artisans, and as political prisoners and their retinues. They were in fact the progenitors of the group we know today as the Cape Malays. The four main arrivals – in 1667, 1727, 1737 and 1749 – wove a distinctive pattern into the fabric of the Peninsula and its life style. What has become known as the Cape culinary tradition owes much to them; the style known as Cape Dutch architecture even more; and it was their descendants who, first as hired-out slaves, later as emancipated freemen, were the skilled artisans – the bricklayers and plasterers, carpenters and cabinet-makers, metal-workers and potters – whose talents gave permanence to the physical structure of the town.

These Malays were a fascinating amalgam of people, and though the bulk of them arrived as slaves the settlement at the Cape also provided the authorities in Batavia with a conveniently distant place of exile for political dissidents or other trouble-makers. Best-known of these was Sjech Yusuf (or Sheik Joseph, as he is remembered today) whose *Kramat* near Faure is one of the six Muslim 'holy places' which ring the Peninsula and, according to many Malays, protect the area from natural disasters such as earthquakes. The Sheik, a brother of the Sultan of Macassar and said to be a direct descendant of Mohammed, led an uprising against the Dutch in Java in 1683 and after a year's remarkably successful guerrilla activity was captured, tried and exiled to Ceylon. But even here his presence was too close for comfort as far as the VOC officials were concerned: his reputation for devoutness threatened to become a rallying-point for the Javanese and others who wished to shrug off the Dutch yoke, and rumours of an uprising to free the Sheik (to lead what in effect was to be a *jihad*) persuaded the authorities to transfer the exile to the Cape. His ten-year Singhalese incarceration ended in 1694 when, with his retinue of wives and personal servants, he arrived at the settlement in *Tafel Vallei* where his reception seems to have been more that of a mogul than that of a criminal. Both father and son Van der Stel accorded him the sort of respect normally reserved for senior dignitaries from Holland or Batavia. He died in 1699, but the five years he spent at the Cape imprinted a purpose and direction to the Malay community which have been followed since then.

The first party of Malay slaves arrived in 1667 – other large groups were to follow between 1727 and 1749 – casual in the practice of their faith, and even in retaining their cultural heritage. The advent of Sjech Yusuf led to a spiritual revival which stemmed as much from his example as from his teachings; a fairly lax Muslim community was so transformed that in the decades to come the Peninsula was to become known as the 'Mecca of the South'. And even though the emphasis of their religious observances eventually switched to Jeddah and Mohammed's Black Stone, some of the eastern origins of their creed remained in such rites as the Chalifah.

The impact of the Muslim faith was largely confined to their own people: until the late nineteenth century, services were held in private homes, and the mosques with their minarets which dot the Peninsula today are relatively late

86

87

Recent years have seen an upswing in both the social and economic fortunes of the urban Coloured community as a whole. Higher incomes and a generally improved status in the business and commercial world have enabled many to move to the 'mini-cities' of Atlantis and Mitchell's Plain, though others still prefer the close-knit communal life of rent-subsidised blocks of flats such as these near Elsies River (85). And some the new wave of prosperity has passed completely by; careless of this, and epitomised by these youngsters hauling scrap on their rickety cart (86), their lives trundle on from one lacklustre day to the next, with a weekend break made bright, perhaps, by a family outing and a roadside picnic (87).

89

architectural expressions of their beliefs. It was as house slaves that these people of the East were to have a broader impact, for their contribution to the Cape's cuisine is recalled in an aroma of exotic spices and herbs every time bobotie, frikkadels, blatjang or samoosas are served.

Many of the early Dutch officials were employed by the Company in Batavia before being transferred to the settlement at the Cape, and had acquired a taste for the oriental dishes – the rijstafels and nasi gorengs – that were standard fare in Goa or Macassar. And they brought their tastes with them. The advent of Malay slaves in increasing numbers led to a subtle blending of the locally available ingredients (and some imported goods) with the skills of these cooks to create the mouth-watering dishes which are the hallmark of what has come to be known as the 'Cape culinary tradition'. It is a unique blend of Europe, the Orient and Africa – often all in one dish.

Yet if it is to the taste-buds of the present that the most lastingly memorable contribution of these eastern slaves was made, they offered other, even more tangible, expressions of their skills: as splendid artisans they gave to the Cape the execution of much of its finest architecture and furniture. Fortunately, when slavery was abolished here in 1834, these skills were not lost and the emancipated Malays continued to ply their various trades.

Despite Barrow's remarks to the contrary, slaves generally were vital not only to the development of the Peninsula and the Boland but eventually to the growth of the Colony as a whole. Without them, agriculture would have come to a standstill: the free burghers and their *knechts,* or paid servants, could not have maintained their farms, let alone have expanded them into the vast productive estates which were to mark the hey-day of the Cape's early wealth. The *knechts* (many of them Germans who exchanged the poverty of the Teutonic peasantry in a Europe constantly torn by wars for service with the Company and later with its former employees) through diligence or marriage (for there seems to have been a plentiful supply of landed widows) eventually farmed for themselves; and a few saved enough to set up as tradesmen in their own right. Their assimilation went almost unnoticed – a far easier and gradual process than that of the Huguenots, whom the settlers of German origin far outnumbered. But there was no cultural mark as such, and the first significant Teutonic impact on the Peninsula and its vicinity did not occur until the late nineteenth century. German settlers had already imposed their thorough orderliness on parts of the eastern Cape near East London when, between 1878 and 1886, there was a substantial influx of Hanoverian farmers to the Cape Flats. Settling in the vicinity of what is now Philippi, these newcomers intended to establish dairy herds, as indeed they had been expressly encouraged to come to the Cape to do. But the sandy, infertile soil provided poor grazing and most of the immigrant party were forced to lay aside their cattle farming ambitions and turn to wood-cutting and harvesting the dense stands of the wattle which covered much of the area and was in constant demand for the fires of the growing city. A stubborn few stuck it out and found that while the former seabed of the Cape Flats with its fast-draining soils would not provide pasture, the addition of compost and mulch could encourage it to produce bounteous crops of vegetables – provided always that the patches were adequately protected from the searing winds. Wind-breaks had long been a fact of life in the more exposed parts of the Peninsula, particularly in summer when south-east winds blow 'which, from this strength and dryness are found to be deleterious to vegetation'.

Gourmets argue that the crunchy carrots of the Philippi farmers, their crisp lettuce, and tomatoes with a tang that Transvaal growers can never attain, stem partly from the Cape Flats soil and partly from the liberal quantities of kelp that the early cultivators incorporated in their fields . Certainly the flavour of a freshly-picked Philippi tomato, the bloom still on the fruit, is incomparable.

Of course vegetables had long been grown in the Peninsula – its origins as a refreshment station had seen to that – and almost a century before the Hanoverians' arrival Barrow was to write: 'The market is likewise tolerably well supplied with most of the European vegetables for the table, from the farms that lie scattered along the eastern side of the Peninsula, in number about forty or fifty.' Few of these remain; most have been buried beneath the developing suburban sprawl. Only a few much-reduced pockets, often little larger than the average domestic plot, are still to be found in such parts as Steurhof, Retreat and Lakeside.

Yet it was the farmers of Philippi who provided produce of unique taste by winning back the unkempt bush to create a patchwork of market gardens.

And it is a taste which can be savoured still. The cultivated areas of the Cape Flats are dotted with farm stalls, and though the bulk of the Peninsula's fruit and vegetables comes from growers elsewhere and is distributed initially at the main municipal market, the discerning housewife or restaurateur knows the spots – the lane adjacent to the old Rondebosch Town Hall, the seaward side of Muizenberg subway – where the produce of the descendants of those would-be dairymen turned market gardeners is still sold. A small quantity finds its way to the fruit and vegetable stalls that flank the Grand Parade, but most is still sold direct to the consumer from the bakkies that have replaced the vendors' carts of yesteryear.

Whereas the Teutonic touch on the Peninsula has been uncharacteristically light, that of the Briton has not. Andrew Shillinge and Humphrey Fitzherbert had claimed the Cape and the Bay of Saldania (as Table Bay was known) for James I in 1620. And later on a small group of criminals was marooned on Robben Island, but the imperial urge which would later colour much of the world's maps in colonial pink was still relatively dormant and the 'act of possession' by these two ship captains did not receive the royal stamp of approval. So the Cape went instead to the Dutch.

Since then, ships of the Honourable East India Company had anchored in Table Bay on voyages to and from its economic spheres of influence: in China where it reigned commercially supreme, and India where it vied with the

Night brings a new dimension to any city. A few lone lights may break the dark façades of office blocks, and spotlit shop-fronts catch the nocturnal stroller's eye; but much of central Cape Town dies a temporary death each sunset. Sea Point's flatland (88), busy even during the day, now comes into its own with a double cordon of neon lights beckoning the hedonist to an appetising array of cafés and restaurants (89) which offer the initiate an almost limitless choice of cuisine. Discos and bars add clamour to the nocturnal spell, for in the witching hours of darkness, Sea Point is not only brash but noisy. Yet the city's nightlife offers other, more sophisticated, pleasures and for many an evening's happiness is a visit to the theatre – to see a play at the Baxter, perhaps, or opera or ballet at the Nico Malan (90), home of the Cape Performing Arts Board.

90

French. But it was not until 1781 that Britain gave any thought to possessing the territory which James I had so cavalierly rejected. Then, in one of those rough and tumble wars which troubled Europe for centuries and had at various times driven the German and Scandinavian *knechts* to serve the VOC, Holland and France found themselves in uneasy alliance against Britain. John Company's trade was threatened and, realizing the strategic importance of the Cape, Britain decided to invade – and was driven off by a French fleet.

Fourteen years later, with the fortunes of the Dutch East India Company in the doldrums from which it would never recover, the European political pendulum swung again: France was at war with the Netherlands. William V of Orange fled to England and the Gentlemen of John Company rubbed their commercial hands in glee: this time they *would* gain the Cape. A naval squadron, commanded by Admiral Sir Keith Elphinstone and carrying a force led by General James Craig, headed south and anchored in Simon's Bay. Craig began negotiations with Governor Sluyskens in an attempt to land his troops under the guise of allies of the Netherlands; with Albion's characteristic perfidy he refrained from admitting that both the Batavian regime and the Patriot Party (which had taken control of Holland when William fled) had aligned themselves with France. Somehow the news leaked, negotiations broke down, and on the beach and dunes of Muizenberg the Dutch forces – mainly Hessian mercenaries – prepared to repel the invaders. A few desultory shots were fired, the mercenaries fled, and in one of South Africa's most bloodless battles Britain gained a toehold at the Cape. The burgher militia, disenchanted with their officers, put up as little resistance and on 16 September, 1795 the surrender was signed at Rustenburg House, in the grounds of which Simon van der Stel had established his first nursery of oaks.

Britain had gained the foothold at the Cape which, despite the brief period of Batavian Republic government, she was never entirely to relinquish. What in effect was to become the colonization of southern Africa had begun. Not

Lined by oaks reputedly planted at the instruction of Simon van der Stel, Government Avenue (91) bisects the site of the old Dutch East India Company gardens, whose cultivation gave the first white settlement at the Cape its raison d'etre. As the Free Burghers' farmsteads thrived and fresh produce became more plentiful, part of the Company Gardens were given over to the collection and preservation of botanical specimens. Some of these – including a giant strelitzia collected by Johann Auge and planted here more than two centuries ago – may still be seen, in what has become the municipal gardens, a haven of peace in the city centre. Here squirrels are ever ready to take food from youthful fingers (93), or a church elder may pause at the outdoor tables for refreshment (92) without loss of the dignity his office confers.

91

only did the course of the Peninsula's history radically change, but also that of the entire sub-continent. In many ways the new masters of the Cape were more genial than the VOC: they encouraged trade and territorial expansion and it was not until, on orders from Britain, Lord Charles Somerset introduced English as the only language to be spoken in the law courts that any real friction developed between Jan and John Citizen in the Peninsula. But this process of anglicization opened a rift between the English- and Dutch-speaking peoples which was to widen well into the present century and in some instances – fortunately very few – has not yet completely healed.

Somerset was carrying out his instructions and, as he admired the Afrikaners and they in turn respected him, it is unfortunate that he should have been the instrument responsible for the rift. His unkinder critics condemn him as 'jingoistic' and autocratic, and claim that only the steadying influence of his secretary Colonel Christopher Bird (of Kirstenbosch 'Bird's Bath' fame), tempered his tendency towards extremes. Certainly his spell at Government House (which he extended considerably at the expense of the old Company Garden) was later marked by clashes and controversy, not only with the Dutch burghers but with his fellow Englishmen and even, towards the end of his tenure, with his Deputy Governor Sir Rufane Donkin.

His autocratic tendency was never more obvious than in the opening salvoes of what was to become the battle for press freedom in which he clashed with Thomas Pringle, George Greig and John Fairbairn when he attempted – successfully at first – to censor the content of local journals and particularly the independent *Commercial Advertiser*. Fairbairn, who was as much a thorn in the flesh of the authorities as the earlier 'scribbler' Adam Tas had been to Willem Adriaan van der Stel, was an outspoken critic of slavery, the treatment of the Hottentots and the administration's frontier policy. He took up the earlier cry of the American colonists of 'no taxation without representation', amending it slightly to 'no taxation without consent' and his platform of 'civilization franchises' won him the leadership of the Lower House when, in 1853, the Representative Constitution for the Cape came into being. Yet in his way he was as much a 'jingo' as Somerset and later Rhodes, and the abolition of slavery which Fairbairn so staunchly advocated was to widen even further the rift between the English- and Dutch-speaking citizens of the Peninsula.

The Dutch influence tended to weaken, but did not entirely disappear; and while British merchants and traders grew more numerous in Cape Town – and the coming of industry accelerated their influx – Cape Town and the Peninsula were never to acquire the 'Englishness' which was for many decades associated with Natal. The early melting-pot of history and the force of Africa itself were to see to that, even at the foot of the continent.

Napoleon is said to have described England as 'that nation of shopkeepers', but ask any Capetonian for directions to the nearest 'Greek shop' and he or she will more than likely direct one to a corner café. For the two Mediterranean races which have stamped their mark most noticeably on the Mother City and her suburbs are the Greeks and the Portuguese; unfairly perhaps, they are regarded as the city's minor trading types. And although both national groups – the Greeks are today South Africa's fourth largest émigré community – have made valuable contributions to the professional, business, artistic and culinary life of the Peninsula, both remain synonymous with food shops: the Greeks with cafés (or superettes, as they masquerade today), the Portuguese with fish-and-chips shops, and both vying with the Indian community (in the public eye, at least) as sellers of fruit and vegetables.

Yet both these Mediterranean peoples were relatively late establishing their presence in the vicinity of Table Mountain. The Portuguese were the first to quaff the waters of the Tavern of the Seas, but they were never more than visitors – sailors, missionaries and administrators *en route* to possessions in Africa and elsewhere, or even as occasional slavers or ivory-hunters. But few stayed, there was little intermarriage and so no cultural impact. To Portugal, southern Africa meant Angola and Moçambique.

94

The first record of Greek 'settlement' in South Africa is as late as 1880 when a group of 11 seamen jumped ship in Port Elizabeth and established themselves as farmers in the Eastern Cape under the leadership of the one-eyed and appropriately nick-named 'Cyclops'. Others, traders following the railway line from Delagoa Bay to Pretoria or attracted by the Witwatersrand diggings, moved into the Transvaal, where several served with the Boer forces in the South African War. There is no apparent record of when the Cape Peninsula's life blood was given its first Greek transfusion, but by 1905 there were enough residents, and presumably passing seamen, to justify the establishment of a Royal Hellenic Consulate, and Cape Town boasts South Africa's first Greek Club which opened its membership five years later.

Today the older members of this community remain staunch to tradition; maintain their ties with the little white-washed villages of the Aegean and the families who live there; celebrate weddings, christenings and funerals with retsina and ouzo, feta cheese and olives; and, as they finger their 'worry-beads', talk nostalgically of the Ionian islands and the Peloponnese. But the younger generation is steadily becoming assimilated; and though, as yet, the transformation is incomplete, the day seems sure to come when a politely murmured 'Kali mera' or 'Kali spera' will be met – even in the corner 'superette' – with raised eyebrow and: 'Sorry? That's Greek to me!'

Although smaller, the Portuguese community seems less likely to lose its identity in the melting pot of Cape Town. Possibly it is their religion that forges the stronger link of national identity, for although the hold of the Roman Catholic church on the peoples of the Iberian Peninsula may in recent years have eased its pressure under the thrust of socio-marxism, it has never relinquished. But if seldom admitted, religion remains as powerful a dividing as it is a uniting force among the people of the Cape Peninsula as it was two centuries ago. The strength of religious faith as much as of heritage knits Cape Town's – and South Africa's – Portuguese.

Equally, perhaps even more strongly, bound by their faith are the Peninsula's Jewry who in a reverse local Diaspora tended for many years to congregate in the 'Jewish' suburbs of Muizenberg and Sea Point. Such apparent clannishness led – for a time and among a certain section of the population – to Muizenberg, particularly, being known as 'the land of the waving palms', an offensive appellation referring to the large number of eastern European Jews who had made their homes there and had the habit of emphasizing their speech with physical gesture. Their tendency to cling together – unlike earlier Jewish immigrants to the Peninsula who had integrated with the community as a whole – was understandable: for as well as their faith they shared a further bond – almost all were refugees from the Czarist pogroms which disgraced Poland and Russia especially in the final decades of the nineteenth and first decade of the twentieth centuries. Later they were to be joined by the pitifully few who managed to flee the Nazi holocaust. And their 'Yiddish' culture was to add a colourful verve and vigour to the Peninsula which earlier Cape Town Jewry – mainly English and German merchants and traders – had not been able to provide.

There had been Jewish astronomers and cartographers among those who manned the first Portuguese fleets to sail Cape waters, and men and women of Jewish origin among Van Riebeeck's tiny group of settlers, though they were forbidden to practise their faith, for all VOC employees had to profess the Reformed religion; and – in spite of this requirement – there were substantial Jewish shareholders and even members of the *Here XVII*. But it was not until the second British occupation that a Jewish presence was felt among the diverse peoples of Cape Town, and then its impact was economic rather than cultural. From Germany and Britain, Jews had been forced by the financial aftermath of the Napoleonic wars to seek new opportunities to buy, sell and trade – and in the booming conditions of the time many of them prospered, first as merchants and later on as financiers and bankers. Others – no less prosperous, though on a smaller scale – used Cape Town as a base to travel into

The wealth of differing architectural detail which caps the rooftops of this cluster of turn-of-the-century buildings in Green Point (94) usually goes unnoticed; the eye is caught instead by the startling scarlet exterior of the furniture and basket-ware shop. Less startling – in Cape Town's bohemian circles at least – is the sight of a young woman puffing at a long-stemmed pipe (95), though it was different enough to catch the photographer's eye.

the hinterland with wagons, pack-trains and even solitary donkeys, so that the itinerant Jewish pedlar, or 'smous' became a popular and welcome figure in the distant hamlets and remote farms of the platteland. A few, men such as Benjamin Norden and Nathaniel Isaacs, felt the lure of adventure rather than of fortune and became noted explorers and frontier pioneers. But it was to the economic sector of the growing Cape Town that early Jewry contributed so vitally – as bankers, in commerce and, later, industrial development.

In 1841 South Africa's first Hebrew congregation was established in the Mother City by 17 of the townsfolk who united to ensure 'holding regular services on Sabbath and festivals and maintaining the Jewish religion in South Africa'. Their pact bore fruit and flourished and it was from this seedling congregation that many future civic leaders and statesmen were to be drawn. Later, with the discovery of the Kimberley diamond fields – Cape Town-born Harry Mosenthal was one of the first to recognize their potential riches – and the gold-rich Witwatersrand reef, Jews from many parts of the world were among the cosmopolitan diggers, miners and manipulators who passed through the Tavern of the Seas *en route* to the new treasure-fields. Some became millionaires and returned to Table Mountain's shadow as benefactors of the arts as well as of education – Sir Alfred Beit is so remembered – or to bountifully restore, as did Sir Lionel Phillips at Vergelegen, the richness of our history.

Remarkably – in view of the fact that Africa was more their continent than that of any other of the Mother City's children save the Bushmen and the Hottentots – the last of the cultural tides to lap the Peninsula was that of the Blacks. There had been black slaves, but their imprint was slight and even after emancipation they were absorbed mainly into the rural fields of agriculture rather than the urban life. And those Blacks nearest the Peninsula – the distant Xhosa of the Kaffrarian border – were not to bow to white supremacy until, more than two decades after the legal abolition of slavery, the prophetess

Nonquase led them to the brink of national self-destruction in persuading them to destroy their crops and cattle. In the mass starvation that followed and destroyed the Xhosa might, survivors were forced to seek food and work among the settlers. Even then, few were to reach the Boland and even fewer the Peninsula.

Not until the decades immediately before World War I did a black urban population of any substantial size develop in Cape Town. Then the city's youthful, labour-intensive industries were faced with a problem similar to that of Van Riebeeck and the first free burghers – a lack of manpower, particularly unskilled labour. At first the Coloured population and little-educated 'poor whites' sufficed as industry's hewers of wood and drawers of water – the men who with pick and shovel, barrow and bucket carved the new roads and permanent ways feeding the nascent suburbs; who dug the clay and shaped and carried the brick to build those suburbs and the factories whose employees they housed; who moved the raw materials both in the mills and in the docks, where there was now a thriving ship-building industry.

But soon the supply was not enough to satisfy industry's growing hunger. Blacks were already travelling north from the eastern Cape to seek work on the mines and the industries created in their wake. And now they turned south and west to the promise of the Peninsula's riches, following a trail already blazed by those brought in to supplement the convict work-force on the break-water and harbour walls. Wages were low but their earnings supplemented the meagre income of their womenfolk from the fields surrounding their traditional kraals. Others abandoned their barren acres and brought their families with them. So began a pattern that continues to this day – of urbanized Blacks and what is commonly known as 'migrant labour'.

Their arrival was gradual but steady. At first the newcomers found accommodation in what was already the slum of District Six, later in shanties and hovels on the city-facing slopes of Signal Hill. But as Cape Town grew so did their numbers swell; shanties proliferated on the fringes of the suburbs, stringing out particularly towards what are now Vasco and Parow, and the perimeter of the then young industrial area of Ndabeni. White dwelling needs were growing too and, cramped by the mountains and the sea, were forced to expand towards the Cape Flats and the 'Northern Areas' so that in a suburban *difaqane* – save in the Ndabeni 'location', which was to develop its own parasitic slum of Windermere (now called Kensington) – the shanties were forced ever outwards.

By the mid-1920s, despite the looming shadows of the depression, the situation had reached what was described as 'uncontrollable proportions' (and regarded by one town father of the day as the 'Black epidemic'); and the authorities proposed the development of a modern township. So the concept of Langa – 'The Sun' – took shape to house 5 000 Blacks and eliminate the 'squatters': and in 1927 the first families moved in there. But after the depression of the early 1930s the hungry industrial giant continued to grow – as did its appetite for cheap manpower. And despite utopian plans – haphazard at first, but based on realistic projections since 1952 – black housing has not succeeded in keeping pace with the demands of industry, nor has legislation been able to appease its appetite, so that the squatters' shacks and shanties remain as much a part of the Peninsula scene as do the manicured lawns and homes of Constantia and the luxury flats of Clifton.

Has at least part of the wheel turned its full circle? Are the polythene tents of Crossroads the twentieth century equivalent of the reedmat and skin dwellings of the Hottentots encountered by Antonio de Saldanha? Certainly the Blacks – whether urban, migrant or 'illegals' – complete the cultural kaleidoscope of the Peninsula's population, the people of the Tavern of the Seas.

Concrete bollards bar much of Greenmarket Square to traffic, creating a tree-studded haven with benches where shoppers can pause, buttressed from the push and bustle of the pavements by a swathe of cobbles. Once these rang to the crush of iron-shod wagon wheels and the cries of Malay hawkers bearing their yokes with baskets of fish or vegetables; now a Muslim couple (96) share a shaded moment of tranquility while, not far distant, in the Bo-Kaap a young boy checks his change in the doorway of a Malay quarter shop (97).

97

District Six: Where crime and charity were friends

Day and night its steeply-narrowed roadways were redolent of spicy cooking, as though the aroma of curries, and sosaties, and blatjangs, and sambals had permeated the crumbling plaster and sweating brickwork. And when windless summer heat lay heavy on its lanes and alleys, less pleasant smells rose from the blocked gutters, held there until the Southeaster blew, for the walls and buildings were high. There were few courtyards, fewer gardens; tenement doorways and shallow stoeps were the space for outdoor living of the people of District Six.

By the turn of the century this once-prestigious suburb nestling on the lower slopes of Devil's Peak – its name derived from the six voters' districts which formed the city's fledgling municipality – had become a rat-infested slum. When bubonic plague broke out there in 1901 many of its buildings were razed – only to be rebuilt by speculators over the following two decades. Yet in this mostly jerry-built warren sweeping down from De Waal Drive to Sir Lowry Road small pockets of the old elegance remained, family homes faded now but still tended by house-proud custodians. For more than 30 years, the sprawl was Greenwich Village, Chelsea and Thieves' Kitchen all rolled into one, beneath a patina of souk anonymity and the squalor of a Bombay bazaar. Its earliest name 'Kanal-dorp' had lost all meaning. Coined from 'Kenallaha' (Malay for 'please') it was said to have derived from early days of development when the tradesmen and artisans, who shared the new extension of the town with the white commercial classes, would ask each other for help in building their homes. But in its later, rag-tag guise neither 'please' nor 'thank you' formed part of the vocabulary – at least of the pavement loungers and skollies of the area.

Here, even at noon, policemen patrolled in pairs, avoiding the byways where 'boere' was a bitter expletive and any stranger was eyed with suspicion. As much as New York's West Side and London's East End, this was gangland, where the 'Razor Kittens', 'Alabama Pistols', 'Kilroy Cowboys' and a dozen equally bizarre-named gangs of young and not-so-young hoodlums each had its clearly demarcated territory; where a Friday evening's entertainment at the Star or Alabama bioscopes could end in stabbing, rape or even murder; and where a late-Victorian reputation as a 'cesspool of vice and petty criminality' had swollen to the proportions of a malfunctioning social sewage farm by the 1940s – and continued to grow along with its population.

To many of the inhabitants of what was still known as 'Kanal-dorp', crime was an accepted way of life, in fact, the only life they knew. Children started early as petty thieves and soon graduated to more serious crimes, seeming almost to court arrest; for by some quirk it was the youths who had spent time at Borstal, rather than those whose activities went undetected, who earned the admiration of their peers and adulation of their juniors. By the time they were old enough to appear in the magistrates' or regional courts most of them trailed a history of juvenile offences into the dock with them. And they would disappear for a fortnight, a month, two months or longer through the grim gothic doorway of Roeland Street gaol, with its imitation portcullis and keep-like walls, to emerge at the end of each imprisonment bearing their shaven heads as proudly as any graduation hood.

Even the law-abiding members of this multi-racial sprawl attached little, if any, social stigma to a spell of '*Koningse vakansie*' in the

98. *Bulldozers have razed much of District Six, though here a church and there a mosque remain to serve the small communities that survive along the former slumland's borders and beneath the towering flats which have been aptly dubbed 'the Pepperpots'.*

bleak, grey penal block, perched on the District Six boundary. In an underworld sub-culture with its own amoral code, linguistic usage, symbolic graffiti and totemistic tattoos, criminality was often a family affair in which the pariah was the white sheep. And in such a milieu it was hardly surprising that attempts at rehabilitation, even among the very young, so frequently failed.

A devout Roman Catholic priest, his faith unshaken by more than 20 years ministering to this the most crime-ridden of the Peninsula's parishes, remarked to me sadly on seeing five youths from his congregation sentenced to Borstal for the first time: 'I'm afraid it'll not be easy celebrating mass this weekend – those are the last of my altar boys.' And a sadly experienced, equally world-weary police sergeant added, 'Yes, Father, and I'll bet you a bottle of brandy to a sip of communion wine that they'll be back here almost as soon as they're back in church.' He was probably right, for though the police patrolled 'Kanal-dorp's' streets with caution, the skollies and their elder brothers, fathers, aunts, uncles – sometimes even grandparents – were more often than not brought to book.

There was even a popular and bawdily-versed song whose chorus ran:

> 'Jou bliksem' sê die magistraat,
> 'Jy slaap vanaand in Roelandstraat.'

Yet in spite of its deserved notoriety – and for many decades District Six had a proportionately higher population of criminals than anywhere else in South Africa outside a busy prison exercise yard – evildoers were a relatively small element in the community. The area's most extreme deprecators could put this figure no higher than 20 per cent – roughly 10 000 out of some 52 000 inhabitants when the slum was as its most crowded – and the reality was probably nearer half that number, even taking juvenile delinquents into account. But in the minds of the public, its tail had given the dog a bad name. Yet even in the last decades before the demolishers completed the work which decay and neglect had begun, professional men and women still dwelt there. Doctors, lawyers and teachers, of faiths as varied as the colour of their skins, lived cheek-by-jowl and largely unmolested among the dagga-smugglers and robbers, pimps and prostitutes, the moffies and shebeen-queens.

Tradesmen, too, had their homes here up to the end, often combining their workshops with their living quarters, and so continuing a tradition that stemmed from the days of the true 'Kanal-dorp'. Thus, even in the mid-1950s, a visit to Merrai who made 'high sossiety tshirts vir die quality mense' might entail her spreading bolts of cloth across a table already cluttered with the remnants of breakfast dishes, and a scrabble for patterns among the children's schoolbooks or the yellowing race-cards which her common-law husband consulted in his tireless search for an infallible system. A seemingly guileless ne'er-do-well, he would importune Merrai's customers for a 'two-bob investment on a sure thing'. But they always came back, for she sewed a legendary fine seam and her collars lay perfectly. Skilled silversmiths and cobblers worked in narrow lanes, and the rasp of saw and the tap of mallet proclaimed the presence of deft cabinet-makers.

And there were the shops. Not your modern chrome and refrigerated-counter cafés or brand-name-conscious superettes, but magic caverns, dark and alive with the scent of green coffee beans and spices, where coils of tobacco hung from pegs alongside tyre-soled veldskoens, and tins of Laurel paraffin rubbed shoulders with hessian sacks of samp and boermeal regardless of health regulations. These were the slaamse winkels and the coolie-shops, where sixpence would buy enough Old Cape boiled sweets to tax one's jaws for a day, and cigarettes were sold singly from opened packets of ten – and the smoker untutored in gangland slang might find a request for 'a packet of Pinhead menthol' met with a 'zoll' of dagga.

One such winkel stands out in the memories of all who knew it for its speciality – curried pine nuts, or denne-putte. Other shops, even the street vendors, sold tamaletjies and sweet pine nuts; but this one maintained its solitary recipe and the privileged few (for supplies, prepared in the back-yard kitchen, were limited even in those halcyon days) would munch contentedly on a tickey's worth, passed across the counter in a conical twist of newsprint. The stately Indian matron who ruled both kitchen and counter refused to pàrt with her alchemist formula, though she would happily dispense its product, emerging through the bead curtain from the living quarters at the rear, at the first metallic tinkle of the spring-bell on the front door transom. A flock of almond-eyed children clung to the sweep of her sari, their relative heights a visual calendar of their father's compulsory holidays in tronk, for he was an incorrigible – though not very successful – fence. When not in gaol he seemed to spend his daylight hours in a battered windsor chair, talking quietly of 'Bombay-side' or listening to sitar music on a wind-up gramophone.

Despite his apparent sloth and his wife's sedate dignity, the shop had an air of seedy vigour, as if this latter-day Fagin's visitors left something of their restlessness behind, for at some time or other every knave in the area appeared to pass through the doorway with its rin-tinkel bell. Or perhaps its mix of the respectable and the sinister lent this particular 'coolie-shop' a special magic, epitomising as it did the vibrant spirit of District Six. 'Kanal-dorp' was never the heart of Cape Town, but for long decades was part of its soul, and if sometimes it was the darker part, it was also the most joyously boisterous.

Where the darker side was sensed, the effervescent jollity was brazen, clamouring to be let out, and emerging as music and song wondrously unique to the western Cape. At dawn, in the evening, even deep into the night – whatever the hour, there was a drift of sound, voices joined in off-key song, the wheeze of a mouth-organ. Rutting tomcats might vie with saxophones, the thud of fleeing feet drown briefly the beat of drums, even the tinkle of breaking shop-front glass diminish momentarily the plink-a-plunk of distant banjoes – but always the music won.

In its music – and particularly in its songs, the moppies and the goemaliedjies – District Six disclosed its soul, its better self; and the sorrows and joys these reflected were contagious, spreading to other Coloured communities – to the labourers' cottages of the Constantia vineyards, the corrugated-iron shanties tucked among the Port Jacksons of the Cape Flats, the homes of the Kalk Bay fisherfolk and the farms of the Boland.

The songs – many born in past history, others reflecting history in the making – had a stamp of their own, imprinted in the streets and alleys leading off Hanover Street and brought gloriously to light or cheerfully revived each New Year. For this was the time of Coon Carnival, when in a kaleidoscope of coloured silks and beaming, painted faces, the men and youths – saints and sinners alike – poured from their warren and spread across the city, to Green Point Track, to Athlone and beyond. They marched to the strumming of banjoes, and guitars, and the brazen blare of saxophones. And as they marched they sang, leaving behind alleyways gay with the bunting made of silken remnants of their costumes – all that was to show for three months' work by the local tailors – and forgetting in their gaiety the squalor from which the celebrations had sprung. Traditional ballads, modern pop, were re-wrought, moulded into a sound that was as much part of the Peninsula as the plaintive fish horn.

The origins of many of the *moppies* and *goemaliedjies* are obscured by time. What meaning, for instance, could the gunpowder plot of Guy Fawkes have for little Coloured children? But in 'Jack and Jill' that came to the fore as a traditional fifth of November song which can still be heard throughout the streets of the Peninsula even though fireworks are no more. Gay and lilting, it provided an excuse for the urchins of the district to fill father's cast-off jacket with straw, affix a *mombakkie,* and parade through the suburbs with the 'Guy' perched in an old pram or a soap box on wheels and calling: 'Penny for the Guy, Maaster'.

Another equally popular *moppie* – to be distinguished from the *goemalied* in having a narrative sequence as opposed to the other's disjointed and unrelated verses – was *'Ertjies en Boontjies'* which appeared on the repertoire year after year. This stemmed from the 1920s when the carnival committee, no doubt in a moment of open-heartedness, invited the participation of coon troupes from country districts – Paarl, Wellington and Stambos (Stellenbosch). Like most Plattelanders of the period, these troupes were disastrously antiquated in their dress. They arrived from the country resplendent in out-moded fashions – Oxford 'Begs' in white flannel with 22-inch bottoms; and peeping coyly from beneath this outdated garb were shiny – oh so shiny – patent-leather shoes. This was too much for the local wags, and they perpetuated it in song: *'Ertjies en Boontjies, Jou patent-leather skoentjies. . .'* the Peninsula's coons would sing as they made their way – many the worse for wear after a day's liquid celebration – along Somerset Road and back to their slum.

District Six had long since lost its graces, but it never lacked airs. Barred from the streets and confined to commercialized appearances that lack the spontaneous warmth and fullness of the past, today's Coon Carnivals are pale shadows of the grand exuberance Capetonians once enjoyed. But some of the songs live on, in Heideveld and Manenberg, in Hanover and Ocean View, among the dispersed offspring of their progenitors. And the special sound of the music is still heard, though softer now, in summer when the Christmas bands still carol the older suburbs. District Six has gone, its tradesmen, shopkeepers and its criminals, like its songs, dispersed but remembered. And when it died something of Cape Town died too.

100

*Effervescent spirits, reflected in shining painted faces (**99**), and a sense of joyous movement (**100**) uninhibited and bubbling, marked the Coon*

Carnival – whether the troupes plink-a-plunked their way through District Six, Bo-Kaap or the city centre's streets.

HISTORY'S LASTING FABRIC

'Light and airy family home with fine sea views and fascinating murals; secluded yet convenient to all amenities – running water, fuel and food supplies within a stone's throw. This ideal south-facing summer residence would suit the D-I-Y enthusiast. Present owner moving up on the evolutionary scale. . .' So might today's estate agent describe the Peninsula's first known dwelling.

It is, in fact, Skildergat (better known as Peer's Cave) in the Noordhoek valley, the home, for parts of each year at least, of Fish Hoek Man – one of our Stone-Age ancestors, who led a hunter-gatherer existence in the greater Cape Town area, and even further afield, more than 25 000 years ago.

He had learnt to tame fire, could cleave stone to shape crude hand-axes and scrapers and, as recent archaeological research has shown, he would migrate to and from the sea according to the seasons, the movement of game and the availability of shell-fish. He was in some ways a prehistoric prototype of today's up-country visitors who flock to the Peninsula each summer to enjoy the sun and beaches – though Fish Hoek Man knew no holidays, with only a respite from ceaseless search for food when perhaps a dead seal or even whale was washed ashore on the beach. Then, after driving off the jackals, the strandwolves and other predators, he could feast and fill his belly.

Long millenia later his descendants moved a few kilometres away to the north- and east-facing caves of Trappies Kop which overlook today's picturesque fishing village of Kalk Bay, and which archaeologists have quaintly dubbed 'Dalerose Parlour', 'Signature Cave' and 'Neptune's Cave' – this last still occupied until a few years ago by a Coloured fishing family. The mouths of some of these middle-Stone-Age habitations are still glissades of mussel, alikreukel and perlemoen shells, scattered with the bones of sea-birds and the occasional seal, showing that the descendants of Fish Hoek Man still plundered the rocks and scavenged the shore on their migrations to the sea. But the artifacts recovered from the debris of the caves show a greater skill in shaping stone implements such as finely-worked laurel-leaved blades which would not shame the modern jeweller. And then there is a gap, narrow in geological time but awesome by our standards, during which there are no signs of man's occupation of the Peninsula.

With weapons more sophisticated and a social sense probably better developed, the way of life of the Bushman bands encountered by the first European mariners differed very little from that of the earliest known inhabitants. They, too, were hunter-gatherers. By comparison, that of the Hottentots – though they were classed with the Bushmen as part of the Khoi-San peoples – was a marked upward step on the evolutionary ladder. These clans, whose clearly demarcated fiefdoms divided the Peninsula and its surrounding area into what today might be regarded as 'spheres of influence', were small-scale agriculturalists and semi-nomadic pastoralists. Their dwellings, though mean and far less substantial than those of the Bantu-speaking peoples to the north, had progressed from the caves of Fish Hoek Man and the *skerms* of the Bushmen. Reed mats and skins were fastened over a branch-pole framework to create semi-permanent structures, very similar to those that can still be seen in the vicinity of Steinkop in Namaqualand, yet at the same time as mobile as the teepees of the North American Indians. Thus the first permanent structure – for Janszen's 'Zandeburgh' was as temporary as the wood and sailcloth shacks of the early sealers – was the wood-and-sod fort built by Van Riebeeck's party.

Its people are the soul of a city, and their buildings its fabric which can provide a visible, tangible chronicle of its history. Their form reflects not only the wealth of those who lived or worked in them, but also the occupants' taste – or lack of it. And although many of these stone or brick-and-mortar records have disappeared through neglect or under the pressures of expansion, enough remain to mark the milestones of South Africa's oldest city in its progress through more than three centuries of civilization.

A Cape Town mayor recently remarked that in a growing metropolis it was impossible to 'cotton-wool' buildings 'just because they are old'. But it is to the credit of Capetonians that there are enough of them with a feeling for our his-

102

101 *(previous page). Early morning sun gilds the tops of buildings and the Methodist church spire, which dwarf the Town House whose cupola was once the tallest structure in this part of the city. Then the Town House was the headquarters and mustering point of the* Ratelwag, *or civic constables; now a museum, it houses a fine collection of paintings.*

The last of the day's division bells has rung and the calm of night descends on the Houses of Parliament (103) belying the fierce verbal conflicts which are fought here almost daily throughout each session. The opening of the parliamentary year, traditionally on a Friday at the end of January, is marked by pomp and ceremony, with a mounted police contingent (102) heading the cavalcade in which the State President rides to make his annual speech that marks the sessions's start.

torical heritage to protest – and protest vociferously – against the worst excesses of the 'developers'. They do not always succeed, but they do try.

Before Van Riebeeck left Holland with his tiny flotilla, the *Here XVII* were explicit. 'In order to take possession of the said Cape, and to hold it as a place of refreshment, a small defensive Fort shall be constructed there, which as far as can be judged, can best be situated near the Fresh River,' he was told. And they added: 'That you may better be enabled to safeguard yourself against the attack of all enemies, you will place on each angle of the Fort four iron cannon, which, together with their appurtenances, you will bring to land.'

The cannons with which the first Commander armed the four bastions of his sod fort set a precedent which was to remain unchanged for almost two and a half centuries, and it was not until the Anglo-Boer War that anything other than naval guns were used in the defence of the Peninsula. Even in the early 1950s the coastal battery in which I served was equipped with guns which had originally seen service on armed merchantmen in World War I.

The walls of the first defensive structure were almost three metres high and surrounded a double-storey citadel with walls more than a metre thick, itself surmounted above an earthen cellar which doubled as a powder store and prison. Nor was the quadrangular fort as small as one might assume from contemporary illustrations: nearly 80 metres separated each of the four bastions, named 'Dromedaris', 'Walvisch', 'Reiger' and 'Olifant' after the settlers' ships. In fact it was a fairly substantial structure – the only trouble, as Van Riebeeck's successor Wagenaar regularly complained, was that considerable sections of the earthen ramparts frequently collapsed.

Nothing remains of the homes of the first free burghers. They will have been too busy gaining an existence from the untamed lands to have time to quarry stone, and the chronic lack of firewood precluded the kiln-firing of bricks – a problem which was to recur for many decades to come. Contemporary records seem to indicate that their cottages were also walled with sod and thatched with the reeds which grew so plentifully in the vleis and along the banks of the Amstel. Hippopotamus wallowed in this river (now the Liesbeeck) that formed the boundary between the land which the settlers had claimed and that which remained acknowledged Hottentot territory.

However, restorers at Westoe – one of Cape Town's lesser-known but more gracious homes – found that some of its walls were built of blocks cut from the clay-like anthills, similar to the termite mounds of southern Africa's more northerly regions, which dotted the Cape Flats in a rash of grey pustules well into the eighteenth century. Protected from the rain, these provided durable material for walls, and it is a pleasing conceit that these Westoe walls may have been erected by Thielman Hendricks, the free burgher of Kornhoop on whose lands at present-day Mowbray these 'ant-hill' rooms still stand.

Even Van Riebeeck himself soon realized that his fort would have to be replaced by a 'stone castle', but the ever cost-conscious *Here XVII* seem to have been reluctant to squander any of their substantial profits on such a structure. The gentlemen in Holland had a reasonably justifiable argument – after all, they had no intention of settling permanently in the place. Finally they relented slightly under the bombardment of Wagenaar's complaints and agreed that in future when the sod walls of the Fort fell down such sections could be repaired with brick, always provided that this could be done 'at moderate expense'. Meanwhile Wagenaar was to 'accumulate materials and prepare estimates for the cost of a new Fortification'.

The restoration of Charles II to the British throne – bringing with it as it did the threat of war between Britain and Holland – gave an impetus to the VOC's decisions, and Wagenaar was inundated with instructions, advice, materials – and finally with Commissioner Isbrand Goske, at that stage a cross between auditor and inspector. Nevertheless it was not until January 1666, almost four years after Wagenaar had been ordered to provide costings, that the Commandant laid the first stone of the new 'Kasteel de Goede Hoop'. The anticipated war had materialised, but the initial Dutch successes were such that in October Van Quaelbergen (who had succeeded Wagenaar a few months after work was begun) received a despatch: 'You may discontinue work [on the Castle] until further orders.' At this stage, the walls were less than a metre high, and even today a careful examination of the base of the Castle shows, under the grime of the modern city's smog, a distinct line where the work was halted. And for more than a decade progress on the Castle was affected by threats of war, the alarums of actual war, and the VOC's desire to save money – despite pleas by a succession of Commanders that the stone fortress should be com-

Built of sandstone imported from the English resort town of Bath, and officially opened in 1900, the imposing City Hall still dominates the Grand Parade. But it no longer houses Cape Town's administration: Parkinson's Law and a burgeoning municipality demanded the multi-storeyed civic complex which towers over the Foreshore. However, twice weekly, the Parade maintains a long tradition when temporary stall-holders spread their wares for sale (104). More permanent and equally long established are the fruit and vegetable stalls (105) which line one side of the square, though even these may soon be moved – and with them the lunch-hour card-players (106) – to make way for proposed archaeological excavations.

106

105

In recent years controversy has flared round many of the Mother City's public sculptures – from Sidney Hartley's stolidly pensive bronze of Field Marshal Smuts which broods in the Gardens, framed by the two spires of the Great Synagogue (**107**), to the convulsive grotesquerie beside the Civic Centre (**108**) which one critic has described as 'two giant paperclips in agonised copulation'. Perhaps a century from now the patina of time will make both artistically acceptable – even as orthodox as the bronze infantryman (**109**) who turns his back on sculptural squabbles.

109

pleted. When Goske returned as head of the settlement in 1671 a certain amount of desultory work was carried out by soldiers conscripted for the task, but they proved poor masons and bricklayers, and no sooner had they finished building the powder magazine than it collapsed.

The ramparts were only half completed when, in 1674, the armoury was transferred there and the 'Kasteel de Goede Hoop' was officially designated as such; in November 1677 yet another Commander, Johan Bax, accompanied by his wife, small son and members of the Burgher Senate, trooped dutifully across what is now the Grand Parade each to take ceremoniously a bucket of soil to start digging the moat. But it was not until April 1679 that it could be said to be complete and 'impregnable' – the latter adjective soon questioned, much to the chagrin of the understandably sensitive authorities, and perhaps fortunately never put to the test. Cape Town's castle must be one of the world's few fortifications against which a shot has never been 'fired in anger'.

Is it, in fact, Cape Town's oldest extant building? In recent years controversy has waged over the issue. In view of the time it took a-building, and the fact that both brick and stone, though not abundant, were available, other structures must certainly have taken shape. Even before the foundations of the Castle were laid the first church was built – with wooden walls, but stone-gabled ends. However, whether any of the buildings which predated the castle remain is open to doubt. Claims have been advanced that De Post Huys, a long, low, thick-walled building at Muizenberg, is the Peninsula's – and hence South Africa's – oldest substantial building; and it is suggested that this three-roomed look-out station was planned by Goske, built and occupied in 1673 during the Franco-Dutch war, and that it effectively constituted a VOC 'presence' on the shores of False Bay. This is the view of distinguished researcher and historian, Marian Robertson, who has done much for the preservation of our architectural heritage and was largely responsible for the preservation and restoration of De Post Huys. Others, with a finer sense of romance than of accuracy, suggest that when Simon van der Stel retired to his Groot Constantia estate and no longer received the free fish ration which he enjoyed as Governor, his slaves used the building as a fisherman's cottage to ensure him an uninterrupted supply of food from the sea.

However, archaeologists working on the site during the course of restoration uncovered what appears to have been the foundations of an earlier building – a fact overlooked by De Post Huys protagonists – and Dr J.F. Midgeley, well-known historian of the southern Peninsula, has pointed out that there is no reference to such a building in the Journal of the Council of Policy for the years 1671-74, though maps of a later period clearly indicate a 'Post Huys' at 'Vis

Hoek' following Simon van der Stel's exploration of the bay in 1687. Like so many Cape Town – and South African – controversies, the one over the oldest extant building seems set to continue for years to come.

Oldest building or not, for nearly two centuries after its completion the Castle was the focal point of the Peninsula and so of its history. As the official home of a succession of governors, administrative offices of the VOC, quarters for the garrison, and later (during the first British occupation) the hub of social life, the Castle *was* Cape Town. Here sat the Court of Justice – the notorious 'Black Hole' conveniently to hand and the execution ground within earshot of the walls; here the Council of Policy met – shifting its venue at least once when a wall collapsed during its deliberations; the first school classes were held close by the torture chambers, as the official guides are quick to point out to generation after generation of visiting schoolchildren – much to their amusement and to the discomfiture of accompanying teachers; and here, until the Groote Kerk was consecrated in 1703, were held the church services for the settlement.

It was during the 1670s, too, that work began on the first solidly-constructed slave lodge. Today, known as the old Supreme Court, it houses the S.A. Cultural History Museum – a fitting retirement for this once utilitarian barracks, for where the Castle has seen and made the city's history, this finely-proportioned building at the top of Adderley Street reflects the changes in the socio-political scene over nearly three centuries as does no other piece of Cape Town.

The first slaves were quartered in the old wood-and-sod fort: they were few and the accommodation was more than adequate, but as their numbers increased and the garrison needed more space, they were moved into a barracoon immediately outside the walls of the Fort. Along with the general growth of the settlement, the Company's garden had expanded under the green fingers of Hendrick Boom, and larger gardens necessitated not only a larger workforce, but also that the slaves should waste as little time as possible being marched each day from their quarters near the sea front to their place of work. By building enlarged wood-and-turf slave quarters on the very border of the cultivated area the authorities saved almost one man-hour a day in each slave's travelling time. Soon this lodge became too small and a brick-and-stone structure, to house up to 600 slaves around a central, open quadrangle, was built. It was to accommodate these enforced employees of the VOC for nearly 131 years, during which time numerous extensions and structural changes were made to it.

Following the second British occupation and the Earl of Caledon's decision to sell off most of the former Company's slaves, the building was converted to government offices and the three men who contributed so much to Cape Town's aesthetic charm – Thibault, the architect, Anreith, the sculptor, and Schutte, the master builder – were called in.

Later on it was to provide accommodation for the first Legislative Assembly, but in its new early nineteenth-century guise (little different from today's) it housed among others the Supreme Court and Master's Office, judges' chambers, the Receiver of Revenue, the Bank, the Post Office and the first Public Library. But all this was still in the future; in the 1670s there was far more mundane work to be done.

By now at the Castle there were workshops, granaries and the armoury, and at least in its early days it must all have been rather damp for its walls stood only a few feet from the edge of the sea, and in stormy weather spray and spume were blown over the ramparts. Outerworks and batteries added later (which disappeared long before the network of railway lines feeding Cape Town's old and new stations was laid), helped tame the worst effects of the waves; yet for all its bustle, the dignity of its officials and the orderliness of the garrison, the Castle was almost as mean as the dwellings of the settlement now developing in its protective shadow. Houses were going up on the fringe of the Company's Gardens, along what was to become known as the Heerengracht, and stretching in the vicinity of present-day Strand Street past Wagenaar's reservoir towards the bush-clad slopes of Signal Hill.

110. *Reflected in a vastness of skyscraper windows, the sun's afterglow vies with the strengthening lights of the evening city in a cubist canvas of colour and shadow.*

111

112

110

Long the haunt of Cape Town's pressmen, the Café Royal hardly merits a second glance and is often passed unnoticed in the narrow confines of lower Church Street (**111**). Equally unremarked are the gilt medallions (**112**) which adorn part of the giant Golden Acre complex's façade. Architecturally this is one of the central city's most advanced buildings, but pressures of transport and attendant parking problems in the past decade have led to the development of equally sophisticated shopping centres (**113**) in several of the suburbs.

These homes were simple affairs, often comprising only two rooms and usually with only a single fire-place, which served both as kitchen range and as a source of heat in winter; and, as now, winters could be cold. There were days when Table Mountain changed its Southeaster 'table cloth' for a mantle of snow; weeks when a bitter chill was blown into the air from the coastal ranges, and in one of the few records he has left for posterity Heironymus Cruse writes of 'mountains capped with snow as far as the eye could see'.

The single fire-place probably stemmed from economic necessity: in the early days there was no scarcity of firewood and the settlers hacked down the thickets of stately silver-trees and waboom with an abandon that horrifies the modern conservationist. But from the days of first house-building a monthly tax of two schillings was levied on every chimney in an attempt to reduce the very real risk of fire. Glazed tiles were prohibitively expensive and the mono-pitched roofs were thatched with local reed; many of the gables which later evolved were stepped, not so much for their undeniable aesthetic effect as to allow fire-fighters easy access to burning thatch. And the tax was singularly successful. Even the low thatched awnings which shaded many of the original stoeps declined rapidly in popularity after minor conflagrations.

Little was to change either in the life-style of the villagers – for the settlement could not yet merit description as a town – or at the Castle, until the advent of Simon van der Stel in October 1679. As Commandant, and later promoted to be first Governor of the Cape, he was to leave an imprint on the heritage of the Peninsula and Boland unparalleled by any who were to follow him, and one might well echo Sir Christopher Wren's epitaph: *Si monumentum require circumspice*. But it was not only in the founding of Stellenbosch, that most gracious of all Boland towns, or the building of his magnificent manor house of Groot Constantia, and the rich endowment of the Peninsula's oak trees, which are all attributed to him, that he blessed the Cape. He was able and industrious – and he brought a new spirit to the Castle, that of a *bon vivant*.

By 1689, when the Englishman John Ovington visited Table Bay and was entertained by 'Min Heer' Van der Stel, additions to the Castle – including the superbly proportioned 'Kat', or hall, where official banquets are still held – were already complete. And in *A Voyage to Suratt in the year 1689*, Ovington was to write:

'The present Governor, who lives with his Council in the Fort, is a very kind and knowing Person. His maintain'd grandeur [sic] and lives honourably. His Publick Tables at once know plenty of European or African wines, or Asian Liquors; and whatever the Land or Water, or Air afford in that place, is serv'd up in his Beautiful Entertainments. To complete the Magnificence of which Sumptious Fare, all the Dishes and Plates upon the Board are made of Massy Silver. And before the departure of their Fleets, the Dutch Commanders are all invited to a Publick Repast, where they Drink and Revel, bouze and break Glasses what they please; for these Frolicks are the very life of a Skipper; and the Governor by indulging these wild Licentious Humours, ingratiates with them more, than by anything else he could advise.'

Ovington, who enjoyed his food and drink as much as he appears to have liked using capital letters, became a chaplain to the English East India Company; and though there is considerable uncertainty as to where and when he died, one version has it that he provided the main course for a cannibal 'Frolick' on one of the islands near Sumatra.

If Simon van der Stel lived 'honourably', the same cannot be said of his eldest son, Willem Adriaan, who succeeded his father as Governor in February 1699. History may have been unkind to him, for he was a knowledgeable and innovative farmer who prepared what was arguably an ideal text-book and guide to local agricultural conditions, and his far-sightedness would have brought enormous benefits to the Cape if his efforts had been concentrated on the common advantage rather than on his own good. Unfortunately, he and many of his officials were venal. A certain amount of corruption seems to have been as prevalent then as it is today, but the new Governor and his officials

Vaunting glass and concrete giants cannot dim, rather they enhance the glowing charm and gracious lines of a pair of narrow, gabled buildings (114) which echo those of Holland and bring to the centre of the city a touch of history and a reminder of a more leisurely age. And though younger by many decades, the pillared portico (115) of an Adderley Street bank also evokes a bygone era. . . when horse-drawn trams drew past its doors, or the first automobiles rolled sedately by.

carried it to unprecedented extremes. While Willem Adriaan busied himself and an army of VOC slaves and employees in building and developing Verge-legen, a majestic estate in the Hottentots Holland, his favoured underlings were farming for their own pockets so much private land that they threatened the freeman farmers' livelihood.

This was too much for farmers already chafing under the rigid controls of production and prices imposed by the VOC, and they sent a letter outlining their grievances to the *Here XVII*. Fearing that this alone might have little impact, they opted to follow it up with a strongly-worded petition. And so began one of the less savoury episodes in the history of the Castle.

The task of drafting the petition fell to Adam Tas, nephew of Henning Husing who was the wealthiest of the burgher farmers and, incidentally, the holder of the company's meat-supply contract. Tas was an acknowledged master of a literate but vitriolic pen, as the few remnants of a diary which he kept at the time reveal. He was arrested on February 20, 1706, and with his locked desk, containing the diary, hauled off to the Castle where at his trial six days later he readily acknowledged his authorship of the petition which he and 63 other burghers had signed. Five of the other ring-leaders were exiled to Holland – which did Van der Stel no good at all for they were able to plead their own cause convincingly – and Tas, still with his desk, was incarcerated in the Castle cells, spending a considerable amount of time in the notorious 'Black Hole'. Even today under the glare of a single lightbulb this small dungeon is dank and eerie; but with the light switched off, it is positively claustrophobic and one cannot envy Tas the more than a year he spent in only a slightly better-lit cell and the 'Hole'. Nor can his desk have provided much consolation.

It was not until April 16, 1707 that orders for his release arrived from the Netherlands, and it was to be a further three years before his 'seditious' desk was freed to join the rest of his furniture on the farm which he had renamed 'Libertas', 'Tas is free'. Van der Stel himself left for Holland in June 1707 to answer charges of abusing his administrative powers and, despite a well-argued case published in the Netherlands as *Korte Deductie* – to which Tas replied in a 300-page *Contra Deductie* (1711) – the former Governor was forbidden to return to the Cape, even as an ordinary burgher.

The effects of the petition and the efforts of the five exiles were far-reaching, and from the time of Van der Stel's dismissal not only was the lot of the free burghers considerably eased but all company officials were prohibited from owning land at the Cape – a move that was to curb corruption even if it did not eliminate it. Tas gained something of a reputation for drunkenness and, whether he deserved it or not, is commemorated today on the label of a potent brand of *vaaljapie* popular particularly among the farm labourers of the Boland he served so well.

If the Castle building had its 'Black Hole', its history had moments of 'black' humour too. A succession of indifferent Governors followed Van der Stel, worst of whom was undoubtedly Pieter Gysbert Noodt. Ever standing on his personal dignity, he had made himself particularly obnoxious during an earlier visit to the settlement by demanding his correct, if temporary, precedence in the official seniority order of the administration. He returned to the Cape to take office in 1726 and gained unpopularity so quickly, as a martinet among the troops and a stickler for protocol among the burghers, that even the ever-kindly Ryk Tulbagh – who served under him and himself became Governor in 1751 after 30 years as a VOC employee – could find nothing pleasant to say of him. So harshly authoritarian was his regime that there were whispers of mutiny and, indeed, several desertions.

During the recapture of one such group, four of the soldiers resisted arrest and were sentenced to death – quite correctly in terms of the law of the time – by the unpopular Governor. On April 23, 1729 as the noose was being placed around his neck one of the four called out: 'I summon thee before the Judgement Seat of All-Seeing God, there to answer for the souls of myself and of my companions.' As he heard these words, Noodt collapsed and died of a heart

After long decades as South Africa's architectural Cinderella, the Mother City gave herself a face-lift in the post-war years. Slowly at first, larger and taller buildings rose in central Cape Town; but these were soon eclipsed by Foreshore blocks, and a frenzy of construction saw old landmarks disappear as the dowager was transformed – not always for the better. Today the tower block of the Golden Acre blots out the sky at the foot of Parliament Street (116) and gives doll's house proportions to the adjacent Post Office block – briefly in the early 1950s the city's tallest building. The titan, too, has lent its stately dam a space-age touch in the covered walkway (with its reflection of another growing giant) that feeds the complex from the station parking deck (117), and in the geometric symmetry of steel and glass (118) which roofs its central wall. But night has soothing fingers, and under her ministrations the harsh lines of the Heerengracht are softened and the lights of moving traffic (119) give the Cinderella of the past a brightly coloured modern necklace.

116

120

No modern block could vie with the stately dignity of the Groote Kerk which, with the Old Supreme Court and St George's Cathedral, graces the upper end of Adderley Street. Recognising this, the building at its rear curves gently round the steeple and clock tower (120). Fate – and economic pressures – has been less kind to the handsome sandstone Cathedral whose plans for much-needed extensions were postponed indefinitely soon after the dedication of the 'rose window' (122), though subscription funds were found to finance the magnificent Mountbatten commemorative stained-glass window (121), a later, but equally dignified, addition.

attack, according to Otto Mentzel, a Berlin-born soldier of the Dutch East India Company who was later seconded to teaching duties at the Cape. Mentzel did not arrive here until four years after the event, so his claim is open to question. Still, the Governor did die that day and the chair in which he suffered his fatal attack has become something of a Castle showpiece.

Apart from such minor excitements, the occasional execution, and alarums and counter-alarums of war, life there had assumed a fairly even tenor; as it did in the town itself, where pleasing canals lined many of the streets, trees provided shade from the worst of summer's heat, and orchards brought spring colours to the backdrop of white-washed houses – the latter effect again a constructional necessity rather than the result of the aesthetic taste of the burgeoning population. For it had early been found that bricks from Holland brought to the Cape as ballast for the Company's ships did not take kindly to the extremes the Peninsula's climate threw at them, while local sun-baked bricks could only resist the ravages of winter rain when plastered and coated with a water-proofing mixture of lime and tallow.

The farms of the Boland, the Tokai and the Constantia valleys, and those at Rondebosch, Koornhoop and on the slopes of Wynberg hill, were all thriving; the merchants and tradesmen in the town itself prospered – despite the VOC's tight commercial reins – as wagons trundled along the dirt road past the Castle, laden with produce for the stalls and barter ground of Greenmarket Square; and, by and large, the settlement in *Tafel Vallei* presented a picture of content. True, there were wars in Europe which had an impact on the Cape. However, communications were slow, and the briefer clashes in Europe or the East might well be over before news of hostilities reached Table Bay, although the alliances and intrigues in Europe, so subject to mercurial change, cannot have made the lot of the Governor and his Council of Policy any easier.

When France, and later Holland, sided with the American colonies in their revolt against British rule, the threat of invasion brought in 1780 a French force to support the Dutch garrison. Fortifications, later to become known as the 'French lines', were thrown up and the first of two blockhouses was built at Hout Bay and armed with cannon – former naval pieces – of the Pondicherry Regiment; and briefly the town's streets were abustle with the bright uniforms of French soldiery and their perruqued and debonaire officers. But except for the additional trade they brought, and a scattering of offspring – some from typically swift war-time marriages, others born out of wedlock – they affected little the lives of the stolid Dutch citizens.

Already the settlers at the Cape had been touched by Africa, become a part of it; and in their cultural backwater, little influenced by the mainstream of European happenings, they were developing a style of their own – an architecture and a way of life – which derived less and less from its Dutch, German and French antecedents. Most manifest in the Boland, it was nevertheless noticeable in the town where, for the wealthier citizens at least, life was smugly content. Slaves ran their homes – under the supervision of *mevrou*, of course; and slaves worked their farms or orchards – usually under the supervision of *knechts*. As long as the harvests were good and ships continued to call, there was little wrong with the world which they could admire from the narrow stoeps on which they sat contentedly puffing their long clay pipes. True, there were foolhardy people who ventured across the distant mountains; some came back with tales of huge rivers and vast plains where antelope grazed in their tens of thousands as far as the eye could see; some did not return. What matter? It was enough to stroll each Sunday to church, or to join one's fellow Burgher Councillors at the newly-built Wacht Huys on Greenmarket Square to discuss the price of meat, the state of the roads or to plan the roster of watch patrols whose headquarters were also situated there. For this was the 'Golden Age' of the free burghers at the Cape, an age of blossoming under the benign Governorship of Ryk Tulbagh.

Symbolic of this era was Martin Melck and the buildings in Strand Street associated with this remarkable man. He had come to the Cape in 1746 as a

121

122

117

common soldier of the Dutch East India Company at a salary of nine guilders a month, and within 14 years of his arrival he had won the Company's wine and brandy monopoly, estimated at an annual value of as much as 34 300 guilders – a success story greater in magnitude than most, but echoed by others to a lesser degree in those golden years. He had been a brick-master's apprentice in Memel in Lithuania, and was to put the skills he had learnt there to good use when he built the first road from Cape Town to Rondebosch. He was only about 20 years old when he arrived in Table Bay, but he worked hard in several spheres other than that of soldiering, and by the time he became a free burgher four years later he already owned two farms. Another two years and – like many *knechts* before and after him – he married a wealthy widow. His marriage to Anna Margaretha Hop brought him the ownership of the two 'show-place' farms of Elsenberg and Mulders Valley, and eventually established him as the leading wine and stock farmer in the Cape.

124

Faint streamers of morning mist rise from the sluggish Liesbeek River, the Amstel of the early settlers, not far from the former lands of 'Kornhoop', one of the first Free Burgher farms. Beyond, Groote Schuur hospital (123), site of the world's first human heart transplant operation, sits comfortably against the steepening slopes of Devil's Peak. These slopes too are home, on their southern aspect, to the ever-expanding spread of the University of Cape Town (124) and its serpentine network of access roads. Like its parent city, pressures of growth have led to a mushrooming of new academic buildings, not all of which are in harmony with the original architectural mellowness of the campus.

Like many of the other burghers of German and central European origin, he was a Lutheran – a religion frowned upon if not actively opposed by the *Here XVII* and their servants at the Cape: even the otherwise moderate Tulbagh resisted petitions for a church in which the followers of the German reformer could practise their faith. But Melck, for all his diligence and honesty, could also be devious, and no eyebrows were raised when he began to build a warehouse, even if it had a remarkably church-like domed ceiling, rows of thick rectangular columns and large 'English' sash windows. A swan with wings outstretched – the symbol of Lutheranism – gave patent blessing over the entrance door, and services were soon held there. No action was taken by the Company – either because of Melck's prominence or owing to a mellowing on the part of the Governor – and Tulbagh is said to have told so influential a citizen that whenever he passed the 'warehouse' he closed the eye nearest to it. Eventually, in 1679, the VOC agreed to the practice of Lutheranism, and the church came into its own.

Soon after Melck's death in 1781 work began on the parsonage adjacent to the church on land which he had also donated to the Lutheran congregation. Known today as Martin Melck House, this building – another result of the successful Thibault-Anreith collaboration – is regarded as 'one of the finest examples of 18th century architecture at the Cape and the only surviving example of a typical Cape Town house with a dormer room, or belvedere, with four windows that formerly looked out over the whole of Cape Town and Table Bay'. The scope which this belvedere afforded was not lost on visiting artists of

123

the late eighteenth and early nineteenth centuries and many of the panoramic views of the town which they sketched or painted are annotated 'from the Martin Melck House'.

Before and after World War II it was a popular haunt of artists and theatre-folk, and sometimes the scene of revels that may have caused some local disapproval but will generally have gladdened the hearts of the ghosts of Cape Town's 'Golden Age' – an era which to its citizens must have carried the promise of endless time.

But the first British occupation was to dim such expectations. With the advent of its garrison and administration the town and its still dominant Castle took on a new hustle and urgency. The Castle with Lady Anne Barnard as châtelaine became the centre of a bright social whirl, and although she countenanced none of the 'Wild Licentious Humours' of Simon van der Stel's days, the walls of the Kat resounded with her happy parties.

'It is a palace containing such a suite of apartments as to make me fancy myself a princess when in it,' she wrote of the quarters she and her husband had chosen, 'not an Indian or Hottentot princess, as I have fitted up all in the style of a comfortable, plain English house.' Plain it may have been by Lady Anne's standards, but even today few would agree with her assessment, for she continues: 'Scottish carpets, English linen and rush-bottomed chairs, with plenty of lolling sofas, which I have had made by regimental carpenters and stuffed by regimental tailors. In a week or two I shall invite all who wish to be merry without cards or dice, but who can talk or hop to half-a-dozen black fiddlers, to come and see me on my public day, which shall be once a fortnight, when the Dutch ladies (all of whom love dancing, and flirting still more) shall be kindly welcomed, and the poor ensigns and cornets shall have an opportunity of stretching their legs, as well as the generals.

'I shall not be stinted for room, as I have a hall of 60 feet, a drawing room of 40, a dining room of 20, a tea room of 30, and three supper rooms – in one of

The vast glass and ferro-concrete monster that is the Civic Centre, with its attendant podium floors (125), bulks large on the Foreshore, spanning six traffic lanes of one of Cape Town's major access roads. At the other side of the city the stark monolith of the new Provincial Building soars skywards in unbroken lines (126). Its precision is heightened by the elaborate gables and cornices of a former gracious town house, now restored as shops and offices, whose ambience in turn makes a sharp and unflattering contrast with the sleek modernity of its downtown counterparts (127).

125

which I shall only have supper, and that cold and desultory, with sideboards and no chairs, as I wish to make my guests happy without being ruined by their drinking half a hogshead of claret at every party. Ducks, chickens, etc., they shall have, but as these are £1 a piece, I shall not fly at any of their excellencies. . .'

For those not honoured with an invitation to one of Lady Anne's 'public' days, or any of the other numerous entertainments organized at the Castle, there were frequent horse races at Green Point Common – where the country's first organized sporting body, the African Turf Club, came into being in 1797 – and, later, the promise of an evening's amusement at the first theatre.

This, the brain-child of the spendthrift governor, Sir George Yonge, was intended to provide entertainment for the garrison – and presumably keep them out of the waterfront stews and taverns – and was built on the *Boerenplijn* (now Riebeeck Square), so named because it had become a popular outspan for farmers bringing their produce to the market three streets away. Work on the building, soon dubbed the 'Komediehuis' by the Coloured and Hottentot communities, began in 1799 and, as usual, Lady Anne had a comment: '. . .there is a new scheme with which the Governor is bitten, and which . . .will probably fall to the ground from its not being a well-judged plan. 'Tis a theatre, all boxes, no pit, each box to cost £24 a year. . .'

Initially, the Governor's 'bantling scheme' succeeded and the first performance was given at the African Theatre on November 17, 1800, though with no pit, and boxes at £24 a year, one wonders just how many of the rank and file among the garrison ever supported it. Perhaps that is why it eventually closed, despite the patronage of various governors including Lord Clarendon, and enthusiastic casts drawn mainly from the officers' messes of the various regiments. Following emancipation, the disused building was resuscitated as a school for slaves. Sunday church services were held by a Dutch Reformed minister in the old auditorium. and it gained its later name of St Stephen's Church during one of these, when angered slave congregants stoned the building. Named after the martyr who died a similar fate, it is the only Dutch Reformed church in South Africa to commemorate a saint.

But for Yonge's garrison it was not all entertainment. War was becoming increasingly real, weaponry more sophisticated; and a massive expansion of the Peninsula's fortification was put in hand, the 'French lines' being extended by the building of the King's and Queen's blockhouses, which still stand out on the slopes of Devil's Peak (their walls a perennial magnet for practitioners of graffiti), as well as of the batteries at Hout Bay. And, as far as buildings generally or fortifications were concerned – except for the brief spell from 1803-1806 during which the Cape was administered by the Batavian Republic (and as a Dutch colony for the first time) – the British presence might never have disappeared, for it came back with an architectural vengeance. If the period of Tulbagh's governorship was the Cape's 'Golden Age', that which followed the Battle of Blouberg and the Dutch capitulation, signed in the town's first 'suburb', Woodstock, on January 10, 1806, merits the title of 'the Age of Bricks and Mortar'.

Under the Earl of Caledon, Sir John Cradock and Lord Charles Somerset a frenzy of building erupted. The enchanting complex of Cape Regency cottages on the slopes of Wynberg hill, surrounding the contemporaneously appropriate 'Waterloo Green', date from this period and were built as officers' quarters. The garrison multiplied, partly as a result of the Napoleonic wars, and also as a staging post for troops *en route* to the expanding boundaries of the Colony and the concurrent Frontier wars, but there was a tremendous non-combatant influx as well, of merchants, traders, camp-followers and a plethora of civil servants to turn the wheels of the growing administrative machine.

The severely simple yet mathematically pleasing lines of the Georgian town houses which had marked the first British occupation were swamped in a rash of more florid Regency buildings: their ornamental façades, pillared porches in the neo-classical style, and even wrought-iron balconies, predominate in

Its sails immobilised by the passage of the years and grimed by the exhausts of a constant flow of passing cars, Mostert's Mill (**128**) nevertheless retains the dignity of a pensioner, work done, its rest protected from the traffic of De Waal Drive by the whitewashed walls that once defended the miller's stocks of corn from his own and neighbours' animals. Less than an arrow-cast away, and higher on the mountain slopes, the granite bulk of Rhodes Memorial (**129**) sits implacable. In a wooded setting and distanced from the highway by a swathe of grass and shrub, the quasi-Grecian temple with its flight of access steps and their flanking bronze lions, affords spectacular views of the Tygerberg, Cape Flats and distant Hottentots Holland mountains. Incongruously, the equestrian statue 'Energy' was for many years the advertising motif of a brand of breakfast food.

131

Though each year the vineyards of the Tokai and Constantia valleys shrink in the face of encroaching houses, grapes are still harvested here (130) and wine still pressed. In the heyday of the 'Valley of the Vines', when Cape Muscatel and Constantia jewelled the goblets of European diners, the gracious life-styles of the wealthy farmers was reflected in their farmsteads. The Tokai Manor House (131) dates from this period, though its grander neighbour, the more imposing Groot Constantia (132) has an even longer history. Built by Governor Simon van der Stel, the main homestead is now a museum – though the cellars still operate as such and coopers still ply their craft on the werf behind the old slave quarters.

130

paintings of the period. And the houses spread. Papendorp, as Woodstock was known, had already become a fashionable suburb on the side of the Castle opposite the town itself; now there was further expansion both here and along the lower slopes of Signal Hill in Bo-Kaap, already partly developed but ideally situated for the growing numbers of artisans and lower-echelon tradesmen. Here, too, were to come many of the artisan-slaves following emancipation, to give it their own special stamp and the character which makes the Malay Quarter unique to Cape Town.

While the residential areas were spreading, confined by the mountain and the sea in the direction which they could take, the centre of the town was undergoing an equally vigorous transformation. Shops and warehouses gradually jostled out the houses on Church and Greenmarket squares and, still demanding ever more space, claimed the gardens and orchards which had flanked the Heerengracht.

The Commercial Exchange Building rose as a monument to the increasing wealth that trade was bringing to the settlement in *Tafel Vallei* which had finally been dignified with gubernatorial blessing as 'Cape Town' in one of Charles Somerset's ordinances of 1815 – the first time it was officially referred to as such. Regimental bands played medleys on the recently-named Grand Parade and in the former Company Gardens, where lawns and flowerbeds had replaced the plot of vegetables and other produce won so hard by Boom and his helpers. And as Queen Victoria's empire spread, bringing peace beneath the Union Jack – except, of course, for what became known as her 'little wars' – so the style of architecture which became associated with her name imposed itself upon an urban area now so grown as to verge on cityhood.

Few would call Victorian architecture beautiful, but some of its grandeur is still to be seen in pockets of the older suburbs and behind the many second-hand shops, cafés and dealers that line the upper sections of Long Street; its neo-gothic extremes still dominate the Grand Parade where the City Hall stands guard; and, mellowed by Government House and the oaks of the Avenue, in the Houses of Parliament where a statue of the Empress Queen looks down with stony eyes on passing parliamentarians and bureaucrats.

Today, between the Castle and the Houses of Parliament and around them both stretches a sprawl of concrete, steel and glass: a sprawl spreading further outwards almost daily as the Mother City and 'greater Cape Town' continues to grow. For a city is a living thing, its fabric reflecting the tastes of its peoples. And though pockets of the past remain, they become increasingly hard to find. . . and the ghosts of Thibault and Anreith may yet wryly mock the searcher.

133

Cape Town's contrasting architectural styles are an effective mirror of its past: where the blank façade of the modern provincial block may overpower the spire of the Metropolitan Methodist Church (133), the Italian Renaissance lines of the City Hall (134) and the classic pillared entrance to the Mount Nelson Hotel (137) have a stature which can no more be over-shadowed by modern dross than can the superb Martin Melck complex in Strand Street (138). The future of the many Victorian gems of Long Street (135) or the quaint sloping streets of the Malay Quarter (136) is less certain. Like the old homes of upper Woodstock (140) the shadow of development lies upon them and they may yet follow Sea Point (139) into flatland.

126

138

139

140

The Arts:
Philistines below the Table Cloth?

Cape Town and its setting has inspired innumerable artists, but bred remarkably few; and even among the more modern men and women who have captured the splendours of the city and Peninsula in paint and pen, most are Capetonians by adoption rather than by birth. Perhaps this is as it should be, for the story of the Peninsula's 'art' is serried, broken, and until recent years at least, Capetonians generally had a not entirely undeserved reputation as philistines.

The Peninsula's earliest paintings, from the Skildergat (or painted cave) in Noordhoek valley, are long since gone, vandalized, and were totemistic rather than aesthetic in their concept. Equally, the delicate tools of Stone Age man, though visually pleasing and 'works of art', were more practical than decorative. So it was left to newcomers, the first European visitors, to give an artistic heritage to the land in the shadow of Table Mountain and even this was practical, for the early mariners were interested in charts, landfalls, identifiable geological formations. . . that was as far as their artistic efforts went.

So it was from second or even third hand source that painters and draughtsmen in distant Europe portrayed the early Cape and its peoples: working from mariners' descriptions and seamen's yarns that grew with the telling. And the earliest illustrations reflect this. The Peninsula's mountain massif is there – the Windberg (now Devil's Peak) and the Lion and its rump flank Table Mountain – but their mass is disproportionate, grotesque. Similarly, early portrayals of the Hottentots and *Boesmans* owe more to the popular image of the 'noble savage' than to reality; the karosses and beads are there, sometimes the steatopygous buttocks, but the features are more European than African.

Nor did the early settlers have time for 'artistic frippery'. They noted the beauty of their surroundings, even wrote extolling it, but left little visual record; such sketches as still exist are mainly concerned with bastions, fortifications, dams and watercourses. So again it was left to men and women from Europe – often gifted amateurs rather than professional artists – to 'discover' the Peninsula in oils, water-colours or ink. Some were brief visitors, others stayed for years, gripped by the magic of the Cape and 'working desperately' to capture it on canvas or on paper. Schumacher, Barrow, Burchell, Baines, Ions, de Meillon, even Lady Anne Barnard, left Capetonians a rich artistic heritage, capturing not only the beauty of the city but the spirit of the era which they pictured, so that the modern viewer can sense the 'feel' of a period in a way that no words can evoke.

Their later counterparts have probably been such artists as Caldecott and Russell Harvey, Leng Dixon, William Papas and Tony Grogan who have caught the essence of the Peninsula, but no style or 'school' evolved that could be described as 'Capetonian'.

Yet if there is nothing unique in the Mother City's art, that cannot be said of her architecture. From the earliest days of settlement an architectural style evolved unique to the Cape, reaching its most evocative in the stately gabled homes of the great farmsteads, where slate-grey thatch still contrasts so effectively with white-washed walls. But it is at its finest flowering in a few remaining city buildings beside which their often titanic neighbours seem brash, even incongruous. Such gems, today shining amid the dross of the city, then bejewelled it, and were essentially the work of two men – Louis Thibault and Anton Anreith. By a most happy coincidence both were present in the same place and at the same time, and by good fortune the VOC declared that they should work together.

For nearly 30 years – through the end of the VOC and well into the second British occupation – the work of each complemented that of the other to such an extent that even in their day as much as now their names were almost inseparably linked.

Neither of them came to the Cape to beautify the settlement, nor to fill the rôles they were eventually to play. French-born Thibault arrived in Table Bay in 1783 as one of the military engineers of the Regiment de Meuron, sent by Holland's French ally to help strengthen the Dutch garrison. Certainly the young man, haughty and one of de Meuron's protégés, worked on the 'French lines' – their ugly bastions and buttresses a sharp contrast to his later work. Yet something of his flair must have shone through, for when the regiment moved on, to other threats of war and, eventually, to battles, Thibault remained as official Architect to the VOC and later, under the British regime, as Government Architect. One of his first commissions was to recreate the façade of the Castle's Kat and its balcony; and here he made use of the recently-appointed Master Sculptor to the Company, Anton Anreith. The two had worked together briefly on other minor buildings and they were to collaborate on many more, but their combination here of line, form and embellishment must remain one of their masterpieces.

Anreith, four years younger than the architect, had come to the Cape in 1778 as a company carpenter, one of the band of craftsmen-artisans so vital to the expansion which had already begun. But he brought a feeling for form and depth, an artistic panache, even to his doorways and window-frames. Officials asked him to provide chairs and chests, their wives tabourets and tapestry frames, and in their embellishment his skill with chisel and mallet came to the fore. In 1786 he was appointed Master Sculptor to the Company and as such his love of the ornate – yet expressed in simple line – was given a rein that his earlier craft with wood had never allowed.

A magnificently proportioned set of gates – long since demolished (has Cape Town a philistine heritage after all?) – at the foot of Government Avenue was followed by an even more magnificent pair for the entrances to the Company's zoological gardens. With prosperity and the number of explorers and scientists who for almost a century had visited the settlement and its hinterland, an interest in the indigenous wild-life had developed. Bisected by the Avenue, two zoological sections came into being: one for the predators, the other for birds and herbivores. Anreith's powerful 'lion gates' still stand.

Thibault, the neo-classical influence of Europe still strong in his creative veins, was designing the Cape's first double-storey farmhouses – Alphen and Uitkyk are examples of this period. Where necessary Anreith embellished them. But it was in Koopmans de Wet house and later in the Martin Melck complex that the harmony of their joint efforts is most evident. The styles differ, reflect changing tastes, but these buildings share a pristine beauty that neither time nor grime have been able to mask. Experts vary in their accolades of Thibault's finest work, but in Anreith's versatility of medium it would be hard to better the pulpit and lectern of the Lutheran Church, or the ornate plastered gable of the wine cellar at Groot Constantia.

After Thibault's death in 1815 Anreith opened South Africa's first art school, but none of its students could compare with the master. There have been other architects and sculptors since Thibault and Anreith. Sir Herbert Baker was to design a number of Peninsula homes, manors – and even railway stations – of grace and charm. Under the supervision of Mitford-Barberton and Gustav Schirmer, the little-known Coloured woodcarver Toya wrought wonders of the doors of the South African National Gallery. But none since the emigré engineer and carpenter have stated so vividly in stone and brick, plaster and wood: 'this is the quintessential Cape Town'.

141. *In a glow of light, the modern lines of the Baxter Theatre beckon with the promise of sophisticated entertainment for a population once regarded as 'philistine'.*

THE BOLAND

It was not much to talk about at first, just a polyglot patois of Dutch and Flemish, of Hottentot and French, with a spicing of Malay and occasional, reluctant recourse to English when no other word could be found. Nor was it anything to write home about; no lexicographer had set his imprimatur on its haphazard spelling, no grammarian had established the proper structure of its sentences. Its genesis and youth were verbal, its parentage a marriage of convenience between the settlers and their slaves, and its adulthood was already well established when, in 1928, Afrikaans was accepted as an official language. Yet it had already forged a nation from a welter of varying identities, its perpetuation no mere symbol but an act of faith whose roots could be traced to the first Free Burgher and Huguenot stock.

As the war-eroded fortunes of the VOC declined and their tight commercial grip on the settlement gradually eased, so the fertile richness of the slopes and valleys bore for their owners ever riper fruit – the 'new' patois that became first a verbal (and later a written) expression of a culture and life-style which moved ever further away from its mainly European roots.

The evolving culture was marked both by paternalism and a rugged individualism, reflected and evidenced in a myriad ways and later underscored by an inherent belief that the *volk* were God's chosen. They were hospitable in the extreme, but visitors – especially the effete Englishmen who typified the officer caste and administration during the first British occupation and the earlier parts of the second – were inclined to interpret the rugged brusqueness that betrayed their relatively humble origins, as a lack of manners. It was not. The farmers who developed the Boland may have lacked the polish of contemporary European society, but they never lacked courtesy.

Circumstance shaped the original pattern of their independent individualism. The nearest neighbour was often many miles away, and the burgher and his family, his *knechts* and his slaves were forced into self-sufficiency in many spheres. And as farms were started further afield, a journey to the settlement –

142 *(previous page). Its vineyards bare now and harvesting complete, a sheltered wine farm and its steading blend with the land under an autumn sky which emphasises the slate-grey thatch and limewashed walls that epitomise the Boland's special ambience.*

The clarion call to long, and sometimes bitter, struggle for the recognition of Afrikaans was sounded first in the shadow of Paarl Rock, on whose vast granite slope the Taal Monument commemorates the language's victory (143). And though the modern lines may seem incongruous against the cultural tradition to which the language gave voice, this too perhaps reflects the paradox of Afrikanerdom. For intense individualism and a love of freedom could live side-by-side with the ownership – albeit benevolently paternal – of slaves, whose working day was measured by such bells as this (144), and the rigid, unembellished dogma of Calvinism went hand in hand with an artistic joy that could create the ornate beauty of a fanlight (145), such as this on the farm Hazendal, near Stellenbosch.

143

for supplies, medicine or even to learn the latest news and gossip – became increasingly arduous and time-consuming; so that while for the townsman life was to assume a gradually easier tenor, the Boland farmer was forced to turn increasingly to his own resources or, when these proved inadequate, to those of his neighbours. And it led to a community of purpose that transcended individual national origins. Ultimately it was to find political and social expression in Afrikaner nationhood.

Some concept of this early life-style can be gleaned today from a visit to Worcester's open-air farm museum – especially on one of the 'open days' when men, in the costume of the period, twist the thin ropes of tobacco, press grapes (or distil the fiery *witblitz,* the appropriately named 'white lightning') and slaughter fat-tailed sheep for their meat and tallow, while their women-folk bake bread or make soap and candles as did their forebears almost three centuries ago. Here, too, are replicas of the simpler buildings of the period: a two-roomed farmhouse with its dung-smeared floor; a *kapstylhuis,* simplest of all frontier dwellings; a weighted wooden gallows on which the leather *riems* were stretched; even a water-mill with wooden sluices where corn is still ground between two stones smoothed sleek by centuries of wear.

And where in his language he was prepared to adapt and accept indigenous words and phrases to express concepts, describe things never encountered in his native Holland, Germany or France, so the burgher farmer accepted other, material influences from his slaves, and from the Hottentots with whom he traded – and sometimes fought. In the kitchen east met – and somewhat – conquered – west; in the still-room the indigenous knowledge of medicinal herbs and roots established a pattern of 'Old Dutch Remedies' that continues to this day in the farmsteads of the Platteland and on the shelves of country stores where bottles of *witdulsies* and *rooidruppels* rub shoulders with proprietary brands of aspirin and gripe-water.

At heart this growing culture epitomized the concept of male chauvinism (many would argue that it still does) in a way equalled only by that of African tribalism; and it emerged as a form of tribalism in which the patriarchal head had virtually autocratic powers over not only the direct clan but the servants and slaves as well. The trio of ingredients – individualism, paternalism and chauvinism – made a heady brew, the partakers of which did not take kindly to any authority that threatened what had become accepted as a God-given right of independence. Manifested first in the petition to the *Here XVII* of Adam Tas and his 63 fellow burghers, it was to take the form of other written complaints and of deputations, even the brief political step of declaring independent republics in Graaff-Reinet and Swellendam – and ultimately of the Great Trek. All stemmed from this fierce spirit of independence; all arose primarily in the Boland, within sight of Table Mountain.

Through the implementation of legislation which would diminish the use of Dutch and, later, by abolishing slavery – Britain was the final catalyst in forming an Afrikaner nation, but the process had begun more than a century and a half earlier. And again while Britain attempted to impose her linguistic will on the Dutch colonists, the very men – teachers such as Andrew Murray – whom she employed to do so were to fan the bellows in the forge of Afrikaner nationhood, for they became the step-fathers of Afrikaans.

For much of the period of its early development Afrikaans was regarded as the language of the uneducated, and even when printed for the first time in the *Cradock News* early in December 1860, Louis Henri Meurant (writing as 'Klaas Waarzegger') treated it with good-natured light-heartedness as a vernacular not to be taken too seriously. It was another 65 years before it received recognition on a par with English and Dutch, the parent it was to supplant.

Afrikaans was, and still is, a fast-growing language. Certainly when Britain annexed the Cape for the first time in 1795 the Dutch spoken was already markedly different from the language spoken by Van Riebeeck and his men. But then so was the life-style of the farmers very different from that of the first Free Burghers. In the steadily-expanding western Cape, particularly, their de-

144

145

146. *Its oak-lined streets, a fitting memorial to its founder, have gained for Stellenbosch the appellation 'Eikestad'. And these trees, introduced to the Cape by Simon van der Stel, join with gems of Cape Dutch architecture to make this centre of wine and learning the most visually delightful of all Boland towns.*

scendants – and those of later arrivals – enjoyed comfort and material prosperity undreamed of by their forebears. Further east, along the coastal mountains where 'new' land was being opened up for settlement, hardships echoed those of the early days; but the Boland basked in the same 'Golden Age' as that enjoyed by the town.

When the British returned to the Cape for a second time in 1803 they resumed and intensified their attempts to eliminate Dutch in schools and from all official activities. And after 1814, when Holland officially ceded the Cape to Britain, their efforts became more determined – so that in 1828 English was proclaimed as the sole official language. The struggle to retain Dutch – and thus ultimately Afrikaans – might have failed had not the freedom of the press been assured in the following year. And from 1830 onwards in this new climate of freedom vernacular journalism began to flourish.

And paradoxically it was Meurant's comic dialogues, published as *Zamenspraak tusschen Klaas Waarzegger en Jan Twyfelaar* in April 1861 – the first book printed in Afrikaans – that led to an upsurge in the publication of Afrikaans letters in *De Zuid-Afrikaan* and *Het Volksblad* as well as in other journals in the Cape, Transvaal and Free State.

Further support came from an unexpected quarter when an English-speaking law agent, H.W.A. Cooper, published his serious *Boerenbrieven* under the pseudonym 'Jan Zwaartman'. These had a considerable impact on literary style, but it was not until 1865-66, with what became known as the 'First Phase of the Language Movement', that any positive course or objectives were set. And by then, although the Boland remained the heartland of Afrikaans, the widened areas of settlement and the Great Trek had carried the linguistic battle-front to distant horizons.

Politically, the Afrikaners of the Boland resented the British Governor's obstructionist attitude to the war between the fledgling Free State Republic and Basutoland, and their earlier passive opposition turned to active anger when Britain first annexed Basutoland in 1868, and then the Kimberley diamond fields two years later. At the height of the dispute Jan Hendrik Hofmeyr ('Onze Jan') became owner-editor of *De Zuid-Afrikaan* and used this to promote a national consciousness among his fellow Afrikaners. His primary concern was to have Dutch reinstated in schools, the courts and the administration, but a parallel movement, which had developed in Paarl, argued that the Afrikaner-Dutch identity could only be preserved by adopting Afrikaans as the language of its people.

In 1858 Cape Town-born Reverend G.W.A. van der Lingen founded Paarl Gymnasium, using Dutch as the medium of instruction, and here he was joined in 1866 by Arnoldus Pannevis whose strong Afrikaner nationalist sentiments were to influence many protagonists of Afrikaans, and who spearheaded the argument that the Afrikaner's identity could be maintained only by the recognition of Afrikaans as a language in its own right. His protégé, Casparus Petrus Hoogenhout, who was to become the most important writer of Afrikaans in the years before 1900 and who was then teaching at Groenberg, near Wellington, threw his weight behind the movement.

Pannevis appealed through the columns of *De Zuid-Afrikaan* for the Bible to be translated into Afrikaans, and was supported by Hoogenhout, who further urged the introduction of Afrikaans in schools – a cause he continued to press.

As resistance to Anglicization increased so also did British efforts to suppress Dutch, and it was at this stage that the most ill-starred figure in the struggle for Afrikaans came to the fore. The Reverend Stephanus Jacobus du Toit while a student at Paarl Gymnasium had been strongly influenced by Pannevis. In 1874, now a student at the theological seminary in Stellenbosch, he wrote a series of articles in *De Zuid-Afrikaan*, defending Afrikaans on philological and religious grounds, and following them five months later with a series of seven basic spelling rules for the language.

By 1875, when he became the Nederduits Gereformeerde Kerk minister at Noorder-Paarl, he had been accepted as the champion and acknowledged leader of the Afrikaans movement, and he consolidated his position when in the same year he was the co-founder of the 'Genootskap van Regte Afrikaners'. Asserting that language and nationalism could not be separated, he founded the Afrikaner Bond – a party which would uplift the Afrikaner and play an important part in both political and cultural affairs. His argument fell on receptive ears in the Boland, and branches were also formed throughout the Cape and in the Free State and Transvaal republics. But in one of the emotive upsets which marked – and still marks – the twists of South African politics, he fell into disfavour among his fellow Afrikaners; and in 1899 his name was struck from the rolls of his own creation, the Afrikaner Bond.

On another political front, Hofmeyr had pressed successfully for Dutch to be accepted as the second language in the Cape Parliament in 1882, and for its position to be improved in schools; and by 1884 it was again used in the courts and became a compulsory subject for the lower Public Service examination. Its reinstatement was commemorated by the erection of the Taalmonument at Burgersdorp in 1893, the main inscription reading: *De Overwinning der Hollandsche Taal.* This recognition led to a polarization of attitudes among the former allies. There were those who were quite satisfied with the new dispensation while others, including Hofmeyr, were determined that Afrikaans should have at least parity with English and Dutch.

Union and the South Africa Act saw these two entrenched as the two official languages of the country, but in 1911 Langenhoven, writing in *Ons Land,* called on the public to choose between Dutch and Afrikaans. Elected to the Cape Provincial Council, he carried this argument further and in 1914 successfully pressed for the introduction of Afrikaans in schools.

Momentum continued to increase and on May 8, 1925, the Official Languages Act recognized Afrikaans as an official language in every sense. Half a century later, on October 12, 1975, the Afrikaans Language Monument, which towers up from the slope of Paarl Mountain, was inaugurated, a symbol of the independent spirit which had not only created a language but, from early free burgher stock, had helped to build a nation.

It was a nation forged by gun and plough which far outstripped the quiet valleys of its origins. When the early rugged individualists moved on, forced by their stubbornness and pride as much as by circumstance to answer the wilderness call of the hinterland that they were to open up, they took with them the language and the life-style of the Boland like cuttings of plants to be planted to flourish in some other garden. But the rootstock remained; and with it a rich heritage of well-tended vineyards, of whitewashed dorps and stately farmsteads – a legacy which for all these tough burghers' character has blessed the western Cape with a softness no other part of South Africa can share. In spring when the young green shoots of oak and vine give promise of the summer shade and harvest; in autumn when these same leaves, a russet carpet touched with reds and golds, warn of winter's coming, it seems as if the Boland has been there forever, so deep are the roots the burghers planted, the foundations they laid. Here the richly fertile valleys, the neatly laid-out slopes are neither Europe nor Africa, but a blend of both.

The real Africa begins, shyly at first, beyond the mountains of the south and east. To the north it gives warning of its drier presence in the summer dustdevils of the Swartland and the Sandveld stretching beyond to the droughtlands of the Namaqua, where Simon van der Stel journeyed on his first major exploration to find the 'copper mountains'.

Some three million years ago this semi-desert of sere terra cotta and khaki was a fertile green, flowing with streams and rivers carving the distant mountains and feeding with their estuaries the great lagoon of Langebaan, its floor thick with rich beds of oysters. To the south where Van der Stel and his explorers were to find a littoral of sparsely vegetated dunes, vast herds of prehistoric antelope grazed fertile plains and wetlands and fell to the tooth and claw of the long-vanished ancestors of today's predators – and of others who left no easily identifiable descendants. Their only record is their fossilised remains, in places

Wherever one goes in Stellenbosch history echoes at one's heels and ghosts of the past stand at one's shoulder. So tangible at times is this sense of the past, that the bygone costumes (147), brought to light each year for the Van der Stel Festival, seem superfluous. The brick and plaster of the old powder magazine (148) which, despite its Lilliputian proportions, dominates the Braak, speak their own legends down the centuries, as do the town-house rows (149) of Dorp Street – the town's main thoroughfare and still lined with irrigation channels that once fed long-gone vegetable plots and domestic orchards.

Umbrellared stone pines and the geometry of a Swartland hillside near Darling (**150**) blend in a natural canvas that would have gladdened the heart of the young Pierneef. Beyond these rolling hills, its waters a magnet for a myriad birds, stretches the Langebaan lagoon where flamingoes (**151**) stalk the shallows as they did long centuries before the first whites touched the southernmost shores of Africa. And though the gum trees which make avenues of many Swartland roads are not indigenous, they too convey a sense of timelessness that even a passing bus (**152**) cannot dent or puncture.

150

138

151

152

139

covered and uncovered by the dunes that march and countermarch at the winds' commands. Elsewhere they are seemingly heaped in some prehistoric charnel house of a myriad years ago, and man brings them to the surface as he mines the phosphate riches of the coastal strip near Langebaan. It is then that they mingle with the skeletal crushings of their modern descendants – as bone-meal fertilizer, replenishing the lands.

Ice ages came and went and the climate changed – sometimes with such spectacular rapidity that animals were inundated by flash floods before they could move to safety, sometimes so gradually as to be imperceptible to the denizens of the region – and so, too, did the seas recede and advance. Some five million years ago, when the inward swell of ice-caps melted and oceans rose to make of the Cape Peninsula an archipelago, the sea embraced the lower-lying parts of the Swartland and Sandveld. And when the waters again retreated the vast oyster beds of what had been once a great estuary fed by countless rivers began to die. Today, now million-year-old fossils, the shells are the calcrete carpet of Langebaan Lagoon and part of Saldanha Bay's giant iron ore terminal, where the drift of ferrous dust from the hoppers and carriers coats the waters and paints the black-headed gulls in bizarre shades of red.

To the south, Nature's own colours still reign supreme in spring along the coast. At Bokbaai, where spring tides send the spume almost to the stoep of Groot Post farmhouse, *Dorotheanthus bellidiformis* bloom in a flamboyant riot of colour. Endemic only to the small curve of coast which has given the Bokbaai vygies their common name, these salt-hardy annuals are among the most popular and widely grown of all the Cape's mesembryanthemums.

It was here at Groot Post that Hildegonda Duckett in the late 1800s wrote her *Where is it?* and *Diary of a Cape Housekeeper* which throw such fascinating light on the way of life – and fare – of her day.

Today a tarmac artery bisects the Sandveld she loved, and the leisurely progress of the Cape cart and the wagon is replaced by a frenetic procession of lorries, cars and tankers. The bush-clad dunes whose game found its way into many of Hildegonda's recipes now house the growing labour force for Atlantis, the industrial growth-point which is officially planned to be a future city, but whose critics view as doomed as its long lost namesake. Here, too, construction gangs have uncovered tokens of man's earlier industry. Bulldozers, picks and shovels have unearthed the artifacts of Stone Age Man – the hand axes and scrapers which provide a fascinating 25 000-year contrast to the lathes, drill-presses and welding equipment of today.

Beyond the dunes, awesome in its potential for benefit or calamity, the Space Age lines of South Africa's first nuclear energy plant mars the serenity of the coast, and its thirst for cooling water threatens the denizens of the nearby sea. For scientists believe that the heat generated by the plant will so alter water temperatures as to change drastically the pattern of marine life in the vicinity. Should this prove to be so, it will be a fateful paradox: archaeologists on a 'rescue dig' before the reactor's foundations were laid discovered the remains of animals, already extinct when man first strode these shores, and lost forever in Nature's cataclysmic change of temperature – the Ice Age.

Beyond the dunes, across the bay, Table Mountain stands aloof: for 25 millenia it has watched the ephemeral work of man. . .

154

Spring, with its promise of longer, warmer days, flushes forth the first blush of fruit blossom outside a farm labourer's cottage (153) in a scene that has been repeated in the valleys of the Boland since the first wooden ploughs broke the virgin earth of the sub-continent. It was in these valleys that the injection of a Huguenot work-force gave impetus to growth, their toil and contribution remembered in the memorial to them (154) which stands proud at the head of the Franschhoek valley, whose peaks are capped by winter snows.

155 *(following page). Centred on the town which has taken its name, the fertile Franschhoek valley symbolises the agricultural richness won from an unknown land by the dogged perserverance of the early burghers – founders of a nation.*

◄153

INDEX

Adderley, Charles Bowyer 59
Adderley Street 9, 55, 108, 113, 116
Agulhas Bank 44
Alexander, Henry 33
Alfred (Prince of Wales) 52, 59-60
Alfred Basin/Dock 52, 60, 62
Alphen 128
Amstel River (now Liesbeeck) 23-24, 119
Anglo-Boer War see South African War
Anreith, Anton 20, 108, 119, 124, 128
Arniston 44
Athens (shipwreck) 52, 60
Athlone 99
Atlantis 87, 124, 141
Auge, Johann 90
Baines, Thomas 128
Baker, Sir Herbert 128
Barnard, Lady Anne 12, 14, 15, 85, 120-121, 128
Barrow, John (explorer) 12, 14, 17, 20, 88-89, 128
Bax, Johan 107
Baxter Theatre 89, 128
Beit, Sir Alfred 94
Bird, Col. Christopher 33, 91
Blaauwberg 37, 44, 68
  battle of 121
blockhouses (King's, Queen's) 121
Bo-Kaap 95, 99, 124, 126
Boland, the 54, 78, 83-84, 95, 98, 113-114, 117, 131-136, 141
Bontebok National Park 67
Boom, Hendrik 82, 108, 124
Bowler, Thomas 58
Braak, the 136
Breakwater Prison 57, 59
British occupation of the Cape
  first 20, 46, 54, 120
  second 33, 52, 54, 93, 108, 128, 135
Burchell, William John 20, 33, 128
Burgerwaghuis 117
Bushmen, the 49, 73, 94, 102, 128
Caledon, Earl of 108, 121
Camps Bay 16, 24, 26, 33, 50, 66
Cape Colony 88, 121
Cape Flats 4, 15, 24, 37, 89, 95, 98, 105, 122
Cape lion 17, 23, 60
Cape Malays 50, 74, 78, 87-88, 95
Cape of Storms 37
Cape Point 23, 64-67
Cape Town Festival 9
Castle (of Good Hope) 4, 20, 52, 55, 83, 105, 107-108, 113-114, 117, 120-121, 124
Charles II, King of England 105
Church Square 124
Church Street 80, 111
City Hall 105, 124, 126
Civic Centre 107, 120
Clarendon, Lord 121
Clifton 24, 49, 95
Coloureds, the 37, 49-52, 95-96, 98-99, 102, 121
Commercial Exchange 57-58, 124
Constantia 24, 51, 95, 98, 117, 124
Constantia Nek 17, 24, 33
Constantiaberg 24
Coon Carnival 98-99
Cradock, Sir John 121
Craig, General James 90
'Crossroads' 95
cuisine, Cape 87-88, 91
Da Gama, Vasco 44
de Meillon, Henry 128
De Saldanha (Antonio) 14, 15, 24, 26, 95
De Waal Drive 96, 122

Devil's Peak 4, 14, 23-24, 96, 119, 121, 128
Diaz, Bartholomew 65
disa, red (Disa uniflora) 33
District Six 95-98
Donkin, Sir Rufane 91
Drake, Sir Francis 4
Dromedaris (ship) 104
Duckett, Hildegonda 141
Duncan Dock 29, 52
D'Urban, Sir Benjamin 55
Dutch East India Company 20, 33, 37, 40-41, 44, 52, 54, 58, 68, 77, 80, 83, 85, 87-91, 93, 105, 108, 114, 117, 119, 128, 132
  garden 90-91, 108, 124
  zoological gardens 128
English East India Company 113
ericas 33
Eva (Hottentot) 4, 77
Fairbairn, John 91
False Bay 15, 24, 26, 37, 46, 49, 51, 58, 66
fish-canning (industry) 50
Fish Hoek/Vis Hoek 49, 58, 107
Fish Hoek Man 102
fishing (industry) 46, 50-52
Flying Dutchman, the 65-66
Foreshore, the 57, 105, 114, 120
fort (first in South Africa) 104
Free Burghers 80, 83, 90, 95, 104-105, 114, 117, 119, 132-133
French Hoek 85, 141
Fresh River 20, 104
Frontier Wars 121
fynbos 30, 33, 65, 67
Genootskap van Regte Afrikaners 136
George V, King of England 66
Glencairn 66
Golden Acre, the 20, 111, 114
Gordon, Col. Robert 20, 24
Goske, Isbrand 105, 107
Government Avenue 90, 128
Government House 91
Grand Parade 4, 89, 105, 107, 124
Great Synagogue 107
Great Trek 133, 135
Green Point 57, 59, 93, 99
  Common 121
Greenmarket Square 77, 95, 117, 124
Groeneveld (now Newlands) 80, 82
Groot Constantia 107, 113, 124, 128
Groot Post (farm) 141
Groote Kerk 108, 116
Groote Schuur (estate) 33
Hanover Street 98
Heerengracht, the 20, 59, 108, 114, 124
Here XVII 37, 40, 42, 55, 78, 83, 87, 93, 104-105, 114, 119, 133
Hofmeyr, Jan Hendrik 135-136
de Hollandsche Thuyn 80, 82
Hottentots, the 23, 33, 37, 49, 68, 73, 77-78, 80, 82, 91, 94-95, 102, 105, 121, 128, 133
Hottentots Holland 114
  mountains 24, 66, 122
Hout Bay 24, 33, 37, 50, 52, 55-56, 83, 117, 121
Huguenots 83-85, 87, 89, 132, 141
Husing, Henning 114
Isaacs, Nathaniel (pioneer) 94
James I, King of England 68, 89-90
Jews (in South Africa) 93-94
Kalk Bay 23, 37, 46, 49-52, 55, 58, 98, 102
'Kanal-dorp' 96, 98
Kasteels Poort 20, 24, 33
'Kat' 20, 113, 120, 128
Khoi-San, the 73, 102
Kirstenbosch Botanical Gardens 30-33
Kloof Nek 29
Kolbe, Peter 46

Koopmans de Wet House 128
Kornhoop 105, 117, 119
Kramat, the 23
Lady Anne Barnard's Pool 33
Langebaan 136, 138, 141
Langenhoven, C. J. 136
Le Vaillant, Francois 20
legends 12, 14, 23, 65-66, 136
Libertas 114
Library (first Public) 108
Lichtenstein, Martin 78
Liesbeeck River 80, 105, 119
Linnaeus 30, 33
Lion's Head 4, 12, 23, 128
Long Street 124, 126
Lutheran Church 119, 128
Maclear beach (Cape Point) 65
McClear's Beacon 17
Malay quarter see Bo-Kaap
Malays see Cape Malays
Martin Melck House 119-120, 126, 128
Melck, Martin 33, 117, 119
Melkbosstrand 37
Mitchell's Plain 87
Mitford-Barberton, Ivan 128
Mostert's mill 83, 122
Mouille Point 50, 52
Mount Nelson Hotel 126
Mowbray 105
Muizenberg 40, 46, 51, 63, 66, 89-90, 93, 107
  Battle of 90
Muslims 52, 73, 87, 95
Neptune's Cave 46, 49, 102
Newlands 24, 79
Nico Malan 89
Nieuwe Haerlem (ship) 37
Noodt, Pieter Gysbert van 114, 117
Noordhoek 23, 49, 56, 102, 128
Observatory 124
Old Supreme Court 108, 116
Oude Kraal 49
Paarden Eiland 40, 124
Paarl 99, 132
  Noorder 135
Parliament, Houses of 102, 124, 136
Parliament Street 114
Pearson, Prof. Henry 33
Peer's Cave 102, 128
Penny, Joshua 15-17
'Penny Ferry' 37
Phillips, Sir Lionel 33, 94
Pier (Cape Town) 55, 57
Pierneef (artist) 138
Platteklip Gorge 12, 14, 20
de Post Huys 107
Post Office, old 108
  new 114
'Post Office' stones 68
Pringle, Thomas 91
proteas 30, 32-33
Ratelwag (town guard) 54, 102
Rhodes, Cecil John 20, 23, 33, 91, 124
Rhodes Memorial 122
Riebeeck Square 121
Robben Island 17, 23, 37, 41, 68, 89
Roeland Street gaol 96, 98
Rogge Bay 50
Rondebosch 24, 33, 89, 117, 119
Rose Street 73
Round House 20
Rustenburg House 90
St George's Cathedral 116
St James 51-52, 58, 63
St Stephen's Church 121
Saldanha Bay 42, 49, 141
Saldania, Bay of 89
Salt River 40, 124
Sandvlei 102
Sceptre, H.M.S. (ship) 15
Sea Point 23, 68, 89, 93, 126
Seal Island 46

Sheik Joseph/Sjech Yusuf 87
ship-building (industry) 95
shipwrecks 37, 40-44, 52, 54-55, 57, 59, 65
Signal Hill 4, 23, 28-29, 95, 108, 124
Simon's Bay 40, 46, 49, 52, 58
Simon's Town 58, 63, 65
Sir Lowry Road 96
Skeleton Gorge 24, 33
slaves and slavery 23, 78, 80, 87-88, 91, 108, 117
Sluyskens, Abraham 90
Smith, Sir Harry 59
Smuts, Field-Marshall J. C. 107
Somerset, Lord Charles 33, 91, 121, 124
S.A. National Gallery 128
South African War 60, 93, 104
Southeaster (wind) 12, 14, 20, 37, 58, 82, 96, 113
Stellenbosch 84, 99, 113, 134, 136
Strand Street 108, 117, 126
strandlopers 44, 46, 49, 73
strelitzia (crane flower) 32, 90
Swartland, the 136, 138, 141
Taal Monument 132, 136
Table Bay 12, 15, 17, 23, 26, 37, 40-41, 44, 46, 49, 52, 54-55, 57-58, 60, 62, 66, 68, 78, 84, 89, 117, 119, 128
Table Bay harbour 37, 52, 54, 59-60, 62-63
Table Mountain 4, 12, 14-17, 20, 23-24, 26, 30, 33, 63, 91, 94, 113, 128, 133, 141
  cableway 12, 24, 26
Tablecloth 12, 14, 20
Tafel Vallei 10, 20, 37, 41-42, 46, 68, 77-78, 82, 87, 117, 124
Tas, Adam 91, 114, 133
Thibault, Louis 20, 108, 119, 124, 128
Thunberg, Carl 33, 40
Tokai 24, 61, 117, 124
Town House 102
Toya 128
Trappies Kop 46, 49, 102
Trautmann, Jacob 50
Tulbagh, Ryk 30, 33, 114, 117, 119
Twelve Apostles, the 24
University of Cape Town 33, 119
Van der Stel, Simon 46, 84, 87, 90, 107-108, 113, 120, 124, 134, 136
  Van der Stel Festival 136
Van der Stel, Willem Adriaan 91, 113-114
Van Hunks 12, 14
Van Meerhof, Pieter 77
Van Plettenberg, Joachim 33
Van Quaelbergen, Cornelis 105
Van Riebeeck, Jan 17, 20, 24, 37, 44, 46, 49, 68, 73, 77-78, 82-83, 93, 95, 102, 104-105, 133
Van Riebeeck's Hedge 33
Van Zurwerden, Hendrik 83
Vasco da Gama Peak 64-65
Vergelegen 114
Victoria 52, 124
Victoria Basin 37, 60
Wagenaar, Zacharias 20, 104-105, 108
Wellington 99
Westoe (historic house) 105
whaling (industry) 46, 49, 50, 68
William of Orange 90
wine 15, 63, 83-85, 113, 119, 124, 134
Woltemade, Wolraad (hero) 40
Woodstock 16, 121, 124, 126
Woody Ravine 21
Worcester 133
Wren, Sir Christopher 113
Wijndberg see Devil's Peak
Zandenburgh (fort) 37, 102